Posted in the Past

Revealing the true stories
written on a postcard

By

Helen Baggott

D0112918

First published 2019

Stourcastle Books
www.stourcastle.co.uk

© Helen Baggott

British Library Cataloguing in Publication Data.
A catalogue record for this book is available from the British Library.

ISBN 978-1-9161070-0-7
Printed in Great Britain

For all the families – *branches of the same tree*

Contents

Introduction   1
Posted in the Past   5
What's Next?   263
Index of Names & Locations   269
About the Author   279

Introduction

There are many books written about postcards – locations, themes, the photographers, the artists who painted the images – but there are very few that look at the messages and the people who wrote and received the cards.

The idea to write *Posted in the Past* found me by chance. Years ago my parents bought two postcards at a car boot sale. There was a connection with the First World War, and the satisfaction of researching those cards and ultimately sharing that research with the family of a soldier killed in that conflict fed my desire to carry on with new projects. That simple act of buying those postcards has ultimately inspired me to write this book.

Many of the postcards in this book were sent in the first decade or so of the 20th century. I was able to tap into the 1911 census and, if the recipient was living with their family, discover their ages, how many children had been born (living and dead), how long the parents had been married, their occupations, and the names of anyone living in the house on that day in 1911. Of course, that wasn't always enough – a snapshot can never tell a complete story. Also, some of the subjects of my research were boarders or employees – with no real connection to the family at that address. Those postcards were particularly challenging to research.

Creating a family tree for each postcard took time – but it allowed me to often trace the sender of a postcard – auntie, uncle, brother, sister were the clues that led me to solve the puzzle. Sometimes I even connected a courting couple to a later marriage.

What makes the 1911 census so valuable is that it's completed by the head of the household. It's a precious moment, seeing their handwriting, and if you are considering researching your own tree, the 1911 census might provide you with something more than the family's facts. I was able to match one postcard's sender to a household purely by the handwriting – of course, that meant creating another family tree for that postcard.

Once I had the proper foundations of a tree – checking as many facts as possible – I reviewed the trees created by other researchers. I never accepted anything from those trees that I couldn't confirm myself. I was surprised at the lack of information some had – and the errors. However, many of the users hadn't accessed their accounts for years – certainly not since the 1939 register was first available. Do my trees contain errors? I hope not. My focus has been on the immediate family and I am confident that those details are an accurate reflection of the families mentioned in this book. If I have come across a query that wasn't possible to resolve, I have either omitted it from a story, or presented it as it is – a genealogist's problem that requires deeper research.

It's such a shame that I found so many incomplete trees – where the creators had abandoned them, for whatever reason. Researching a family's history is a rewarding hobby and if you've begun yours and struggled, why not revisit it? There are new records becoming available all the time and you might suddenly find that missing link.

The various census returns that are available show a person's age on that day. Therefore, some tolerance must be allowed for the year of someone's birth. Only the 1939 register lists a person's actual date of birth and very few of my subjects were alive or traceable in 1939. I was able to use other records to further my research – including baptism and marriage records – and they improved the accuracy of a person's year of birth. You will find more information about those resources and the various census returns at the end of this book.

There are many genealogists out there with far more experience and knowledge than I have. The tips I include are not written for them, they're for those who have begun a tree and stalled, have watched and enjoyed *Who Do You Think You Are?*, or seen any TV programme that focuses on our more recent history, and thought about their own backgrounds but never really got started.

A number of the postcards have led to wider research. As well as the stories behind the individual postcards, you will read about how the people connect to events of national and international importance. Even the shorter stories – perhaps just dates and occupations – have a place in our history. They are the customers of the grocers, the children of miners, servants to the rich; branches of the same tree.

I have not included any family trees in this book. Although the trees I created were essential to my research, it's the stories behind them that I am sharing. With the exception of one postcard, I have not brought any family into the 21st century. Most stories end well before the Second World War – not because I am unable to find them, but because it's unnecessary to reveal any information beyond this time. Please contact me if you would like any information about a family.

There are no words that I can write that adequately convey the emotional impact of a death. Sometimes I have worked through a person's life with great swiftness, arriving at their death before I've appreciated that life. I know how losing her father at a young age affected my mother and I hope that anyone reading this book will appreciate that I haven't researched a person without considering how they might be affected by a death – of a young child, a soldier, a beloved parent.

In the index are any names and locations mentioned in the stories. Please do not get excited at the appearance of Arnold Schwarzenegger. To the best of my knowledge, he is not related to any of the families. However, he is associated with my research.

Although my focus is on the messages, I have also included the images. I know most readers would want to see both sides of the story and often the image provides another insight – especially with fashion and transport. I have created a blog where you can see colour versions of the cards and you will find more information about this on page 279.

The words written on the postcards do not belong to me. Most were written by people who remain unknown. Without those words I would have no book. I thank those people who wrote the cards and those who received and kept them.

Most of the postcards have survived for more than one hundred years. The recipients have kept them, treasured them – even those with the mundane messages about train delays and bad weather. Decades later, for whatever reason, the postcards have been discarded. For the time-being, the postcards that form the stories in this book are in my safekeeping. They connect me with our collective past in a way that is unlikely to be achieved by our emails, tweets and Facebook comments.

I hope you enjoy reading about the people I've researched and that it inspires you to look at your own history.

Posted in the Past

Dec. 1913.

Dear Gillie.

Just a few lines to wish you a Bright + Merry Xmas + a Happy New Year.

Pte. G. Freeman
No. 16373.
25th Grenadier Guards
Chelsea Barracks
London
England.

001125

001125

8

001125
December 1913
Pte. G Freeman
No. 16373
25th Grenadier Guards
Chelsea Barracks
London
Dear Gilbert
Just a few lines to wish you a bright & merry Xmas and a Happy New Year.
CF X

1927
Mrs Freeman
Queens Road
Stonehouse
Gloucestershire
Just a little bird to bring you my very best wishes for a very happy birthday. Don't be too gay – or eat too many 'goodies' – I wish I could pop in & see you, but my present is always at home – no one can [?] away with that & I hope you will get lots of comfort from it – so with love & many happy returns from Dora.

When I was deciding the order for the postcards and their stories, I knew I had to begin with these two cards. They were bought by my parents and became the inspiration behind what would become this book. I began the research 20 years ago and the final discoveries were made in 2018.

The oldest card was sent in 1913 to a soldier in the Chelsea Barracks and included his service number – 16373. I soon found that Gilbert Edmund Freeman (b.1891) had been killed in the First World War. That information came from the Commonwealth War Graves Commission website. The other card was sent 20 years later to his mother.

At the time that seemed like the complete story – I didn't have access to any genealogy sites and I don't believe I was even working on my own family's tree. Later, using Ancestry, I decided to look at Gilbert's family and began by creating his tree.

His parents, William Osborne Freeman (b.1855) and Matilda Freeman née Teakle (b.1860), were married in 1888 in Gloucestershire. Matilda was William's second wife. His first wife, Emily née Bodman (b.1857), had died in 1884. They'd had one son, William Osborne Freeman (b.1878). In the 1881 census the family were living in Freshford, Somerset. William senior was employed as a manager of a flock manufactory and they lived in Mount Pleasant – a row of terraced cottages for workers at the nearby Freshford Mill. In 1891, William and his second wife and their children are shown as actually living at the mill.

Freshford is a pretty little village. If you've seen the Ealing Comedy film *The Titfield Thunderbolt* you might recognise the area. The village scenes were filmed in Freshford.

When I visited the village I was struck by how quiet it was. It wasn't designed for modern transport and I parked outside of the village and walked in. I soon found the mill. The roar of the water announced why the area had so many mills along this stretch of the River Avon. Although it's now been redeveloped, the derelict buildings I saw indicated how large a business the mill had been. In fact, Freshford itself is quite an industrial village. The former brewery's chimney dominates the landscape.

According to the various census returns, William and Matilda had five daughters and three sons. All but one was born in Freshford or nearby Woolverton: Mary (b.1888), Charles (b.1891), Lucy (b.1892), Gilbert (b.1894), Vincent (b.1895), Dora (b.1897), Irene (b.1900). Ruth (b.1903) was born in Stonehouse, Gloucestershire.

Woolverton is one of those places that's little more than a cluster of houses. It's now cut in two by the busy A36. Although I was unable to locate the actual house, I did spend some time wandering around the lanes that lead away from the main road.

In 1898, William, Gilbert's half-brother, married Mary née Swain (b.1875) in Monmouthshire. The 1901 census shows them in Staffordshire with William employed as a gardener. They lived in a cottage with another gardener.

Sometime before 1911 – perhaps even before 1906 – the couple had moved to Saltash in Cornwall with Charles, Lucy and Gilbert. William owned a shop and traded as a seed merchant.

With the help of the Saltash Heritage Centre I was able to locate the shop and they even had a photograph of William standing outside the premises at 97 Fore Street in approximately 1906.

By the time of the 1911 census the family had moved to a larger shop – 87 Fore Street. Over the years the shop continued to trade and at the time of its closure in 2004 it was a general hardware store, still run by the family.

The card sent to Gilbert in the Chelsea Barracks was from his brother Charles who had emigrated to America before the First World War and he would eventually become a naturalized American citizen.

Gilbert's younger brother Vincent also enlisted and served from January 1916. Later, he would join Charles in America. Both brothers can be traced to Massachusetts. Their parents eventually returned to Gloucestershire (some time after 1901) and lived in Stonehouse – as did the children that had not moved to Saltash with their half-brother.

Family members appear in passenger lists – sailing to and from New York. In 1926, Dora and her mother are listed as a teacher and housewife, respectively, and living in Stonehouse.

Gilbert was killed on 16 September 1916 in the Battle of the Somme. He has no known grave and is remembered on the Thiepval Memorial in France. The listing for Gilbert, confirmed by his service number, contained the references to the section on the memorial where his name and rank (private) can be found.

In 1927, Dora sent the postcard to her mother in Stonehouse, postmarked Canterbury.

In 1930, the family returned to England from a trip to America and were listed as: Matilda (housewife), Dora (teacher), Irene (shoe fitter), Ruth (teacher). Dora is listed as living at Stourmouth Rectory, Canterbury. Her mother and sisters are shown as still living in Stonehouse.

That could have been the end of Gilbert's story. However, in 2018 I decided to have another search – just to see if any new information had been shared. Like many communities, Saltash has compiled a record of the town's soldiers who appear on their First World War memorial. The information held by the Saltash Heritage Centre mirrored my own. I also found a mention of a Gilbert Freeman in the Chalford Parish Local History Group's record of the 156 men on their war memorial – which includes Gilbert as Private Gilbert Freeman. That group had made their research available online and I discovered a photograph of a group of soldiers taken in the Chelsea Barracks. Some of the soldiers had been identified and one of those was a Gilbert Freeman. The photograph was included in a letter sent home by another soldier, Wallace Clissold (killed in 1914). He wrote of 'going to church with Osborne Freeman's son'. The document adds that 'Osborne Freeman's son was Gilbert Freeman'.

Was that the Gilbert Freeman I was researching? I was told that the details had been meticulously researched and their Gilbert was the same one. I was directed to another site that had a photo of Gilbert. They were not the same soldier. Apart from there being no likeness, I was concerned about the rank – Gilbert is recorded at Thiepval, Saltash and Chalford as a private and this new Gilbert was a lance corporal.

Gilbert also appears on the war memorial in Stonehouse, where his parents lived. He is recorded there as a lance corporal. Could the memorial at Thiepval and the research at Saltash and Chalford be wrong?

I decided to recheck all the online records I'd seen and came across a new document – Gilbert's Medals Rolls Index Card. Gilbert's rank was originally entered as Pte. It had been smudged out and changed to L/Cpl. – in the same handwriting as the main entries. Was he promoted shortly before his death? I believe so.

I knew that Gilbert was based in the Chelsea Barracks around the time of Wallace's photograph (Charles's postcard was dated December 1913 and Wallace, who wrote the letter home, was killed in September 1914).

Wallace's service number is the final piece of the jigsaw – 16371. Gilbert's service number was 16373. I knew that Gilbert enlisted in Stroud. Perhaps that's why Chalford claimed Gilbert for their memorial.

Considering Gilbert's story complete I decided to share my research online – wondering if any of Gilbert's relatives might search for him. I had decided that it would not be appropriate for me, a complete stranger, to approach any family members. Within hours I was contacted by descendants of his brothers who had emigrated to America. Comparing their photos with the one of Gilbert in the barracks photo was an unforgettable moment. The likenesses were uncanny.

A few weeks later the heritage centre in Saltash contacted me. Another family member had visited Saltash seeking information. My research was passed to them and they got in touch. They now have copies of those original postcards and they have sent me family photos and two postcards sent by Gilbert to his parents.

Throughout my research, my motivation was in remembering Gilbert – a stranger, not a name in my own family tree. Gilbert and his fellow soldiers fought for people like me. Sharing his story doesn't repay that debt, but it is a personal act of remembrance.

How did those original postcards find their way to a car boot sale in Dorset? I have no idea. However, Gilbert's sister Mary died in Bournemouth in 1975.

The research and outcome of Gilbert's story was beyond my expectations. Twenty years ago I was satisfied just to discover what had happened to him. Today, there are so many additional records available that research has become far easier. What follows are more stories – not all are as detailed as Gilbert's, but they form part of our history.

A.D. NINETEEN FIFTY

"I see the War Babies' Battalion is a coming out."

002122

13

002122
France
Monday
11 November 1918
Mrs T Russell
PO
Pembridge
Herefordshire
England
My Dearest Mum
You will be pleased to know that I am having a great old time. Have just arrived in a decent little town. Here the civilians are terribly excited and of course very happy. It's fine to see people merry and full of life. I guess you are very excited at home now –
Au revoir.
With fondest love and kisses, I remain ever your affect. son.
Tommy

This is the only postcard that doesn't belong to me and I am indebted to its owner for allowing me to include it.

Although Tommy/Thomas appeared in a very detailed tree on Ancestry – one that included newspaper clippings and photographs – I needed to create my own profile and not just import that information. There's no satisfaction in simply accepting someone else's research – especially without checking it.

I'm glad I did this because I discovered at least one error. Thomas Russell was born in 1897 and one document attached to his details for his army enlistment showed him as Thomas Reginald Russell. A search of the birth records over a slightly wider range confirmed this to be a different Thomas born in 1896. I can appreciate how the error was made. What are the chances of there being two Thomas Russells living in Pembridge at the same time? However, the middle name was the clue – there are no other records that give any second name for our Thomas.

On the tree, Thomas is listed as Tommy. As you'll discover if you do your own tree, listing your family with their registered name is essential – even if you know they were never known by that name. If that researcher had confirmed the name, I'm sure they wouldn't have mixed in Thomas Reginald Russell's record. Also, the address given in the army records is for Market Square and our Thomas lived in East Street.

Just to be satisfied that my own research was correct, I decided to create a new tree – for Thomas Reginald Russell. I wanted to prove they were two different people. They both had entries in the 1901 census returns at different addresses and with different families. Yes, there were two.

In 1911, Thomas Reginald was a boarder at Bourne College in Quinton, Worcestershire. By 1939 he had survived the First World War, married and

14

become a baker and grocer. Fortunately our Thomas was the post office overseer and would presumably not have confused the names! Undoubtedly, given their respective locations, they would have known each other.

So what of our Thomas? He was born in 1897 and had three sisters: Sissie (b.1900), Elsie (b.1906) and Ivy (b.1910).

Thomas married Minnie née Smith (b.1904) in 1934. I knew from the postcard that his parents, Thomas (b.1874) and Alice née Howard (b.1871), ran the post office in Pembridge. In 1881, our Thomas's grandfather, Charles Russell (b.1843), ran a grocery business in Market Square. That sounds familiar, doesn't it? In 1901, I had found Thomas Reginald living with his grandfather Charles Russell – then a retired grocer. The tree had come full circle. Thomas and Thomas Reginald were cousins.

The hints created by Ancestry were almost overwhelming. I decided not to add any of the information they suggested to my own tree. However, I did review that other tree again. I couldn't find Thomas Reginald – and he should have been there as a cousin.

There are a lot of documents added to Thomas Russell's profile – mainly family photographs and newspaper clippings. I know they belong to my Thomas because they mention his occupation. A local newspaper reported on his community spirit and how, at the age of 79, he was awarded the BEM. Thomas had left home to work in Leominster as a sorting clerk and telegraphist. During the First World War he was a wireless operator. He returned to Pembridge in 1942 – where he lived until his death in 1977.

POST CARD.

THIS SPACE MAY BE USED FOR COMMUNICATION
IN THE BRITISH ISLES, ETC.

THE ADDRESS ONLY TO BE
WRITTEN HERE.

16 JUL

16 JUL

I am sending you
a picture of a garden,
as we have been disap
pointed about sending
the real flowers this
week — there has been
so much wind & rain.
My daughter thanks you
for letter received & letter
we are so sorry you
have been more suffering
lately. E. M. Oldfield

Miss Mabel Cushing
11 Vernon Street
Broughton
Nr. Manchester

The Garden, Shakespeare's Birthplace, Stratford-on-Avon.

"There's rosemary, that's for remembrance;
there is pansies, that's for thoughts."—
HAMLET.

664

PRINTED & PUBLISHED BY J. SALMON SEVENOAKS.

FROM AN ORIGINAL WATER COLOUR DRAWING BY C. ESSENHIGH CORKE.

003015

003015
16 July
Miss Mabel Cushing
11 Vernon Street
Broughton
Nr Manchester
I am sending you a <u>picture</u> of a garden as we have been disappointed about the <u>real</u> flowers
this week! There has been so much wind and rain. My daughter thanks you for letter
received yesterday. We are so sorry you have been more suffering lately.
CM Orde Ward

Mabel (b.1876) lived with her mother and three of her siblings in Broughton – David (b.1882), Dorothy (b.1891) and Winifred (b.1894). Mary née Rye (b.1848) was a boarding house keeper. Although it had been ruled through, she had added to her entry in the 1911 census that she had 15 children and that four had died. Her husband, James Cushing (b.1844), had died in 1905 and in the 1901 census he is listed as being a clerk of work. When the couple married in 1864, James was a carpenter – as was his father, James (b.1823). Although Mabel appeared in other family trees, none of them added to what I had already discovered. She died in 1922 – without marrying.

I wondered if the sender of the postcard might add to the story.

I knew the card had been sent from Eastbourne and the surname was Orde Ward. It took only moments to find the family – Clara Mary née Parker (b.1844) and her husband, Frederick Orde Ward (b.1843). Frederick was a vicar and the couple had four children – Cicely (b.1880), Clara (b.1882), Winifred (b.1883) and Aubrey (b.1886). Cicely was born in Australia.

Frederick was born in Hampshire and his father, Edward (b.1810), was also a vicar. In 1871, Frederick is listed as a priest in Worcestershire. Frederick and Clara married in 1878 and a year later they are listed as passengers arriving in Australia. Two years later and they're back in the UK, living in Hampshire.

Although I traced all their children, it's the youngest, Aubrey, whose story demands sharing. I soon discovered that he had died on 11 November 1918. Aubrey spent most of his life in Eastbourne. In 1911, he was living with his family and working as an artistic designer.

I found a record of his medals and they included confirmation of his service details: Lincolnshire Regiment, lieutenant. His death is recorded as being an accident – in Grantham. I found more details in Eastbourne College's Roll of Honour – a detailed list of their 174 men who died during the First World War. Aubrey's entry confirms that after attending the college he went to Wadham College, Oxford. He later became an artist and partner in a colour printing firm. Initially he was refused entry into the army on medical grounds, but was accepted in 1916 and became an instructor in France. After an extended period of ill health spent in a Red Cross hospital in Dorset, he returned to his depot in Grantham. On Armistice Day, when many would have begun to feel a sense of relief, he was killed in a freak accident. A plane, flying too low, hit Aubrey and killed him.

The postcard was sent by Aubrey's mother, Clara – the handwriting is a perfect match to the signature on Frederick and Clara's marriage register.

004001

Love's Own
Sweet Rose.

V.297-6.

POST CARD
Printed in England

Rotary Photo London.E.C.

Rotary Copyright.
Reg Design No 734734.

Chaswyn
26th April 1936
my dearest Winifred.
wishing you very
many Happy Returns of
your birthday, with
fondest love from
Charlie.

Mr W. L Smith.
Chaswyn.
15. Circle Gardens.
Merton Park.
S. W. 19.

004001

004001
26 April 1909
Miss W Purnell
14 Ballingdon Road
Clapham Common
SW
Dear Winnie
Very many happy returns of your birthday – will you thank Mrs Purnell for the kind invite for Wednesday, but Mother and Dad both seem to want me to be at home, so I hope she will excuse me. Can you come in to tea with me instead?
With love from your affectionate friend Gladys.

In 1911, Winnie Purnell lived at Ballingdon Road with her parents, Edwin (b.1864) and Annie née White (b.1864), and her siblings: Edith (b.1890), Herbert (b.1892), Alice (b.1895), Leslie (b.1900) and May (b.1903).

Winifred was born on 26 April 1893 and the postcard's a lovely example of how prompt and reliable the postal service was at this time.

In 1911, her father was an engineer and fitter of sanitary appliances. In later records his trade hadn't changed but he is listed as a plumber. Also listed: Edith as a milliner, Herbert as an electric engineer, and Winnie is a draper's assistant.

During the First World War, Herbert served with the Royal Warwickshire Regiment with a service number of 16809. He was discharged in June 1917 and died in The Pavilion Tankerton Hospital in Whitstable, Kent – a military hospital – in 1920. He was only 28. His medals record shows the address as Ballingdon Road – a useful confirmation that I had found the correct Herbert.

Leslie is listed with the RAF in July 1918 – shortly after his 18th birthday. His identity was confirmed by the inclusion of his father's name as next of kin. In 1939 he is recorded as a civil servant, of national importance, and living in London with his wife. At this time Edith was unmarried and living with her parents in Ballingdon Road. Alice married Leonard Whitticks (b.1893), a shop assistant, in 1921. May married Harry Day (b.1900), a bank clerk, in 1927.

Although the immediate family is recorded mainly in London, Winnie's mother (Annie née White) was born in Broughton Gifford, Wiltshire. Annie's father, Skreen White (b.1839), was a publican of The Fox and Hounds pub in Broughton Gifford. In 1891, Annie was working as a barmaid in The Three Lions pub in Holt, Wiltshire for her uncle, her mother's brother, William Deverell (b.1834). The pub closed in the 1980s.

What of Winnie? She married Charles Smith (b.1895) in 1929. At the time of her marriage, Winnie still lived in Ballingdon Road. Her father was now a builder. Charles was a clerk and the couple were married in St Luke's in Battersea.

In 1939 Charles is recorded as working for the Metropolitan Water Board. As I added that information to Winnie's tree, I was alerted that it duplicated information in another tree. Charles appeared elsewhere in my research.

Winnie's postcard had been bought years ago in a small batch from a junk shop in Devon. I picked several from a shoebox that was as damp and musty as the shop itself. In with that batch was another birthday card and until the duplication alert, I hadn't considered they may be connected.

26 April 1936
Chaswyn
15 Circle Gardens
Merton Park
SW19
My dearest Winifred
Wishing you very many Happy Returns of your Birthday.
With fondest love from
Charlie.

When I had originally searched for Charles Smith I had found him living with Winifred and his mother, Jane Smith née Cupit (b.1861).

Winnie and Charles lived in a prosperous area. Walking around Circle Gardens in 1939 I found their neighbours had some interesting jobs: senior sanitary inspector Metropolitan Borough of Chelsea, higher executive officer with HM Customs and Excise, analytical and consulting chemist, retired police sergeant, dance band saxophonist, turnstile inspector at a greyhound track, publisher with the *Daily Mirror*, and chief inspector of the Metropolitan Police.

When Winnie died in 1979 she still lived in the same road and her probate records show her address at number 10. The card was addressed to number 15 and that's where they were in 1939.

Winnie's two cards covered 25 years and they were in excellent condition. Even the damp shop couldn't affect their overall quality. I'll never know how they reached Devon; my only regret is that I didn't choose more because I'm sure I would find other connections to Winnie and her family.

005103

005103
21 July 1905
Miss F Pettit
Post Office
Aughton Street
Ormskirk
Blackpool
Dear Flo
Thanks for letter. Don't forget to write before Friday. Hope you will like this one. Tell me if you have seen anyone that I know. It has been lovely here. No rain whatever. Sorry you have had such weather.
Jessie

Florence Pettit (b.1890) was a post office telephonist, probably operating a switchboard and connecting callers. The postcard was sent to her place of work. However, she was easily traced to her family's home in St Helens Road. Her parents were William (b.1855) and Mary née Wickstead (b.1852). William was a timber salesman. The couple had six children in total, but by 1911, three had died. Living at home with Flo and her parents were Elsie (b.1884) and Esther (b.1896).

In 1851, William's father, George (b.1822), is listed as a mariner and in 1861 he worked as a boatman – possibly employed by the customs service. By the time William and Mary married in 1878, George was a customs house officer. William's mother was Esther née Powell (b.1823), the daughter of a stonemason.

Mary Wickstead's father, Crispin (b.1807), was a shoemaker. Her mother was Mary née Baxendale (b.1817).

Flo – the recipient of the postcard – married George Winrow (b.1889) in 1916. In 1911, George was a chemist's assistant. His parents, Richard (b.1836) and Eliza née Dew (b.1852), ran a boarding house. At the time of their marriage in 1870, Richard was a butcher. In 1876 he placed an advert in a local publication, thanking the 'gentry and public generally for the very liberal support received over the five years' he had carried on the business at 11 Market Place, Ormskirk.

George Winrow, Flo's husband, served in the Royal Navy during the First World War. By 1939 the couple lived in Blackpool where George was a shopkeeper, selling sweets.

What happened to Flo's post office? It was eventually replaced by a modern building in the same street. The original property was redeveloped into living accommodation. An estate agent's online details allowed a glimpse inside – perhaps even showing the room where Flo worked.

Flo would have been one of the first generation of telephonists. She appears in postal service records from at least 1905 as an operator.

THE AVENUE, TRINITY COLLEGE, CAMBRIDGE.

POST ⚓ CARD.

For the British Isles only, THIS SPACE AS WELL AS THE BACK MAY BE USED FOR CORRESPONDENCE, VIDE Post Office Regulations.

THE ADDRESS ONLY TO BE WRITTEN HERE.

Dear A.
        I hope you enjoyed
your holiday. Don't
you think this is a
pretty place, I thought
it would one more for
your collection. best love
        from E.

Miss Wise

High St

Winslow

Bucks

006105

006105
Miss Wise
High Street
Winslow
Bucks
Dear A
I hope you enjoyed your holiday.
Don't you think this is a pretty place, I thought it would be one more for your collection.
Best love from E.

Martha *Anne* Wise (b.1882) was the daughter of William (b.1852) and Ann née Hobbs (b.1857). In 1911, William was a surveyor and sanitary inspector. The other family members living at the address were sons Herbert (b.1883) and Ralph (b.1886), and William's widowed mother, Hannah (b.1829). Herbert and Ralph were carpenter/joiners.

In 1901, Anne was a visitor, staying with a family in Shanklin, Isle of Wight. The head of the household was William Calladine (b.1855), a gardener. He and his wife, Ann (b.1857), were born in Derby. They had lived in Shanklin for at least 17 years.

Anne Wise's father, William, was a stonemason. His father Richard (b.1816) died some time after 1866 and his widowed mother Hannah appears in various records as a lace-maker. The area in Buckinghamshire was known for this industry, with the workers producing lace at home.

Ann Hobbs' father William (b.1828) was an agricultural labourer. In 1871, Ann is listed with her family as a lace-maker – as are many others in their close neighbourhood.

The 1911 census confirms that Anne had six siblings, although three had died. Ralph Wise appears in several overseas records. In 1912 he left England for Australia, sailing from Liverpool. He enlisted in the Australian Imperial Force in 1917. In 1923 he married Evelyn née Dawkins in Australia and the couple returned to England on a visit in 1927. Ralph died in Australia in 1978.

Anne married Percy Johnson (b.1883) in 1915. Percy served in the Royal Army Medical Corp during the First World War. Percy survived the war, but Anne died in the spring of 1918.

Lowestoft from Pier

007108

007108
17 August 1911
Mrs Bazeley
The Nurseries
Twyford
Berks

Will F please make me a shield and send to Danecroft. How are the chicks? Have not heard from Ethel. Please give her my new address.

Had a wash again this morning. Too cold Tuesday and Wednesday and very rough. We have had our characters read they are perfectly true am quite anxious for you to see mine. Please let me know if I am wanted home yet. But shall not stay long as everything is dirty. Love Elsie.

How do you kill a chestnut tree without outward show please? The tree belongs to someone else.

Also send pair white kid gloves longest for Sunday.

Elsie was certainly a busy girl and I can't help imagining her mother smiling with a sigh as she read the card.

Elsie Bazeley (b.1890) was the only child of William (b.1862) and Carrie née Coke (b.1862). William was a nurseryman and he appears in several trade directories at London Road in Twyford. In 1881, he was also working as a gardener. His parents were William (b.1832) and Mary née Benham (b.1835) and they had seven children. In 1911, William senior is listed as a gardener. Also living at home was William junior's brother George (b.1861) – another gardener.

Carrie Coke was the daughter of Charles (b.1834) and Mary née Webb (b.1842). In 1911, Charles and Mary were both listed as being retired china and carriers in Twyford. They had 12 children and by 1911, two had died. In 1871, Mary's brother, Charles Webb (b.1853), lived with the couple and is listed as a gardener. In 1881, Carrie was a housemaid in Finchley. Her employer owned Berwick House in Oak Lane.

Elsie, who sent the card, was living at home in 1911 – just a few months before the postcard was sent. At that time she was 21, with no occupation recorded. In 1919 she married Percival Ford from Yorkshire. He was a metal machinist and the couple were living in Yorkshire in 1939.

There's little doubt that if Elsie's father William didn't know how to kill the tree, someone in her family would – but why would she need to know? Was it a troublesome neighbour? We will never discover that – or why she wanted her father to make her a shield.

Despite trying to follow all of her aunts and uncles – all 19 of them – I was unable to find a match for Ethel. Was she a cousin who had fallen through the census gaps? Possibly.

Selworthy.

Aug. 2?/07. POST CARD
Am still at
Minehead.
FRITH'S SERIES

This Space may be used for Communication.
The Address only to be written here

008014

008014

28 August 1907

Am still at Minehead but not in the same hotel. This is high up and splendid situation. Went on a pretty drive today to Selworthy noted for its lovely alms houses. Splendidly surrounded gardens…old church…

Hope you are better.

The postcard used to illustrate this story is of a pair of cottages that are part of a group that cling to the side of a steep hill that eventually leads to Selworthy Beacon in Exmoor. Unfortunately the writing on the card made it impossible for me to accurately research the recipient. However, the sender was on a trip to the area and mentions Selworthy's almshouses.

I'm indebted to a resident of Selworthy who told me that the lady standing by the front door of the cottage is Mary Eames née Williams (b.1811). So, instead of telling you the tale of the recipient of the card, I am unusually sharing the story behind the image itself.

Although the card was sent in 1907, the original image dates to 1890 and is still available on postcards published by Francis Frith.

According to the 1901 census, Mary was born in Selworthy. However, in the preceding returns she is listed as being born in Widen, Northamptonshire. In 1871, whilst living in Selworthy, she is employed as a needle-woman. We have to go back to 1861, to find her living with her husband, William Eames (b.1805), a carpenter. When the couple married in 1833, neither could sign their names.

William sustained a life-changing injury, and despite losing the use of his right hand, he trained himself to continue woodworking – making tables and chairs. William died in 1870 and Mary died in 1901.

The church register for this time also lists a Thomas Williams (b.1825), 'commonly known as Valters'. Before his death he was living on parish relief at Selworthy with his wife, Charlotte née Morell (b.1815), the daughter of a carpenter. In earlier census returns the couple lived in nearby Bossington and he was an agricultural labourer.

When the couple married in 1860, neither could sign their names. However, the marriage was witnessed by a Mary Eames. Was this the postcard's Mary Eames? If so, by this time she had learned to write.

Why did Mary's place of birth switch between Northamptonshire and Somerset – was that human error or has Mary's true identity been confused with another? William Eames' mother was also called Mary – as was a sister. However, they died in 1845 and 1832 respectively.

009107

009107
Rev S Herbert
Chaplain's House, Royal Academy
Woolwich
Dear Sir
*I have got a furlough & go on the 2nd November God willing. My address then will be 17
Collins St. Northampton. Hoping this finds you quite well & happy.*
Yours sincerely
Ellard

William Ellard (b.1872) and Ann née Lawrence (b.1867) had seven children: William (b.1890), Ellen (b.1892), John (b.1894), Catherine (b.1901), Dorothy (b.1903) and Clare (b.1907).

Both sons and their father served in the First World War. A record maintained by the Northamptonshire Family History Society website lists men who were serving as at 1916. The list was compiled by Northants Record Office and based on records made by the Finance Committee in 1916. The writers of the original list acknowledged that the list may be incomplete. It includes two names for 17 Collins Street: William Ellard (sergeant 10th Cheshire) and John Ellard (sergeant RFC). William senior served in the 10th Cheshire and died in 1916. I believe the postcard was sent by William – the eldest son. Some records indicate a William Ellard from Northampton served in the Grenadier Guards – which would fit with the cap badges in the image. In 1911, a William Ellard is listed in a barracks in Caterham. I also found John Ellard listed in barracks in Pirbright.

Ann Lawrence – the boys' mother – was one of 14 children. As I added her siblings to the tree I was concerned I had mixed in another family. However, Ann's mother, Mary (b.1849), had included the number of children she had given birth to in her 1911 declaration – despite Ann's father, Joseph (b.1844), dying in 1905.

According to William and Ann's marriage register, Ann's father was a confectioner and this is confirmed through the other available records. From at least 1871, Joseph and Mary Lawrence lived in St Giles Street, Northampton where they ran a confectionery business. In 1861, Joseph was at another address in St Giles Street – living with his brother John (b.1835) who was also a confectioner.

Online images show that J Lawrence & Co Ltd's name is clearly visible beneath the windows of the St Giles Street premises. A trade directory from 1914 lists the business as 'confectioners & bride & birthday cake manufacturers'. Although the business did change names, it remained a bakery and confectionery business until relatively recently.

I'm sure the sender of the postcard is in the photograph. It's frustrating not being able to confirm who it might be.

UNCLE TOBY AND HIS WIFE FOR SALE

POST CARD

The Address to be written
on this side.

Miss Kate Owen
Fort Terrace
Dursley
Glos

010065

010065
2 December 1911
Miss Kate Owen
Fort Terrace
Dursley
Glos.
Dear Kate
I received your PC alright. I expect I shall be up home for Christmas. I hope the wedding went off alright. You will be losing all your brothers now just how are they getting on at the Crown now? I am enjoying myself alright down here I have been to another part to my other brother well dear I will now close with love [?]
My love to George.

Kate Owen (b.1896) lived with her parents Alfred (b.1856), a machinist, and Elizabeth née Whittard, housekeeper (b.1856), and siblings Andrew (b.1887) a turner, Llewellyn (b.1891) a grinder for petrol engines and George (b.1895) a machine hand. Kate was a cloth picker. Alfred and Elizabeth had 12 children and one had died by this time.

The 1901 census provided more details about the children and I was able to add Florence (b.1879), Laura (b.1883), Arthur (b.1889) and Emma (b.1893) to the tree – making eight named out of the 12.

The 1891 census revealed more: Alfred (b.1875), Herbert (b.1878) and Charles (b.1881).

With so many siblings, I knew this would be a complicated tree to develop and I left the children and focused initially on the parents.

In 1871, Alfred was living in Wales as a boarder. It was a relatively large household and Alfred was a coalminer. Throughout all the records, Alfred is listed as being born in Gloucestershire, as he was in 1871. Ancestry provided many, many hints relating to Alfred and I slowly worked my way through them – sticking with those most relevant to the direct family. With so many children, many of the hints were connecting the family via baptisms and marriages.

Once I'd finished reviewing the hints I looked at another online tree. I found one that had a different maiden name for Elizabeth. I had Whittard and found one with her as Hancock. This is explained by her first marriage – to William Whittard (b.1850). That tree included another child – from the first marriage: Sidney (b.1872). Selina (b.1887) is also listed (with her second husband as father) – making Elizabeth's total children discovered as 13. Selina died a few months after birth – tallying with the 1911 census.

From the records of her first marriage, I found that William was a mason – as was his father, James Whittard. Her father, Sidney Hancock (b.1829), was a labourer.

It wasn't possible to research all of the parents' siblings – so I looked in more detail at their children. Andrew and Llewellyn had married just after the 1911 census and I'm sure it's these brothers the sender of the card is referring to as being lost. The postcard mentions The Crown – was a relative the publican?

I found Charles had become publican at The Crown with his wife, Fanny (b.1879). The pub's building is now a restaurant – although there is a pub of the same name, further along the street.

What became of Kate? She married George Evans (b.1895) and the couple lived with their family in Sutton Coldfield. George was the son of a metal roller and the family lived mainly in the Aston area.

In the postcard's message, a George is mentioned – would it be the man who would become Kate's husband or was it her brother? Kate married in 1921 – 10 years after the card was sent.

The General Register Office for England and Wales (GRO) was founded in 1836 by the Births and Deaths Registration Act 1836, and civil registration commenced in 1837 – Wikipedia

011026

011026
September 1912
Mr J Wood
2 Railway Terrace
Station Road
Dorking, Surrey
My dearest Pa and Ma
Just another card I thought you would like one of these, I am just off to the gospel [?] it has
been a lovely day here quite hot plenty of people about, not much news, we went for a drive
in a brake to Preston and through a place called Sutton on Friday. It was lovely we had our
dinner on a beautiful hill covered with heather.
Much love from Jim

James Wood was born in 1861 in Kent and was the son of William Wood (b.1837), a railway labourer. By 1881, he had left home and was living as a boarder, working as a railway porter. Ten years later and he lived with his wife, Harriet née Buttenshaw (b.1860), and their children in Surrey. By now he was a railway signalman. Later, in 1911, he was a railway porter.

The couple had 11 children and by 1911, five had died. Ernest (b.1886) was a domestic chauffeur in 1911. By 1939 as a widower, he was an owner-driver of a hired car. Mabel (b.1888) worked as a nurse (domestic). In 1911, she and her sisters, Annie (b.1885), a cook, and Ruth (b.1893), a housemaid, worked in the same home for a secretary to public companies in London. Herbert (b.1901) would become a bus driver.

Unfortunately I wasn't able to trace who sent the postcard. The sons I had found had no middle name and a search from the year of the couple's marriage didn't find a Jim. I had only found eight of their children – Jim was one of the missing three.

012092

012092
November 1905
Miss M Reffell
Manor Farm
Horton
Slough
It is nearly time for post so good bye.
Frank.

There are quite a few gaps in the story of this card. However, I do at least know who sent Madge (b.1895) the card – her brother, Frank (b.1892).

Frank and Madge had a sister, Eileen (b.1894). In 1911, she was an art student and lived with the family in Horton.

Their father was Joseph Reffell (b.1859) and he was the son of a farmer – Raymond Reffell (b.1819). In 1871, Raymond farmed 275 acres and employed 10 men, five boys and four women. Their mother was Emily née Perkins (b.1866) and she was the daughter of a farmer.

Madge married Philip Bayley (b.1895), a dentist. He was the son of a hosier – Frederick (b.1864) and Edith Bayley (b.1866). Frederick's father was William Bayley (b.1835) and he was a farmer of 900 acres and the employer of 25 men, 10 boys and six women. In 1939 Frederick and Edith lived in Slough. Also with them was their married daughter and a son – a hosier.

Isn't it typical of a brother to fulfil an obligation to write, but only just? Madge can't have been too upset – she did keep the card.

ILFRACOMBE, LANTERN ROCK & COAST

013005

Rugby III v Northampton
Sat. match
begin 3-30
Recreation Ground

R. Reeve

26-3-09

G. C. Andrew Esq
21 Pennington St
Rugby

013005

Thatcher Rock, Torquay

Wishing you all a
very happy Xmas
& bright New Year.
Hope you are all well.
We are very busy, but
will Ann. Xmas.
J. Baker.

Mrs Andrews
Glen lee
Grosvenor Rd.
Ripley
Derby.

013005

013005
Miss K Andrews
Glenlee
Grosvenor Road
Ripley, Derby
Dear Kathie
We shall be pleased to see you and Vera on Monday. Will you come here yourselves as we shall be unable to meet you.
Yours Aunt

26 March 1909
OC Andrews
21 Pennington Street
Rugby
Rugby III Northampton Sat. match begins 3-30.
Recreation Ground.
R Reeve

22 December 1911
Mrs Andrews
Glenlee, Grosvenor Road
Ripley, Derby
Wishing you all a very Happy Xmas & [?] New Year. Hope you are all well. We are very busy, still.
Love
J Bacon

I began with the 1911 census and found Kathleen Andrews (b.1896) living with her parents George (b.1857) and Annie née Clarke (b.1865) and a sister, Vera (b.1899). George was a dental surgeon and also living with the family was Stephen Madden (b.1892) a dental apprentice.

Octavius Charles Andrews (b.1867) was George's brother and is listed in the 1911 census as a classical tutor. He lived at the Pennington Street address in Rugby with another brother, Alfred (b.1855) – a clergyman.

The Andrews family was possibly one of the more complex that I came across during this project – complex because the family's history had already been carefully researched and the information available was almost overwhelming. However, I decided to remain focused on the postcards and work from them.

Kathleen was born in Ripley and her baptism records confirm that her father was a dentist and that the family lived in Chapel Street – also confirmed in the 1901 census.

She appears as a passenger in several registers and I first found her in 1925 as a schoolmistress, sailing to Port Said for work in Palestine. A year later, Kathleen married Cyril Reading in Amman, Jordan. There's a wonderful photograph attached to the tree prepared by another researcher of the couple's marriage – complete with guests in their traditional Jordanian clothes. Later, Kathleen appears in other passenger lists – in 1933 sailing to Egypt with two of her children, and in 1937 returning to England from Egypt.

Cyril Reading (b.1882) was born in Northamptonshire. In 1939 the couple lived in Essex and Cyril is listed as a retired colonial service fruit farmer.

Vera, Kathleen's sister, married a bank accountant. Another sibling, George (b.1902), died in infancy and there's a touching note attached to Vera's profile in Ancestry. It's an image of a small toy that had belonged to George that she had kept. I found that immensely moving – especially when I discovered that George had died on Christmas Day in 1907. He had, according to a memorial card, suffered from measles for 19 days.

Annie – Kathleen's mother – was the daughter of a publican. Before her marriage, all her census returns show her with relatives. Her father, William Clarke (b.1836), died when she was only five and her mother, Isabel née Banks (b.1837), died eight months after Annie's birth.

Who was the aunt that sent the postcard? I couldn't find that either parent had a sister. The postmark is for Nottingham. The Clarke family – Kathleen's mother's family – lived in Nottingham and are found there in 1871, and I believe the aunt belongs to this branch of the family.

What became of Octavius? He appears in the 1939 register – as a classical tutor at the same address in Rugby.

SHAKESPERIAN COTTAGES, BROADWAY.

POST CARD.

THIS SPACE AS WELL AS THE BACK
MAY BE USED FOR COMMUNICATION.
(Inland Postage only.)

THE ADDRESS ONLY TO BE
WRITTEN HERE.

Having a ripping
time, etc. etc.

Love.
G.E.

Miss Stafford,
Typing Dept.,
40. IV.
Local Government Board,
S.W.

014077

014077
2 June 1914
Miss Stafford
Typing Dept.
40 IV
Local Government Board
SW
Having a ripping time, etc. etc.
Love GE

When I bought this card, it was really for the message – it's such a brief and tongue-in-cheek message to send to someone, perhaps a colleague. It never occurred to me that I might trace Miss Stafford. However, I had to try.

I began my search using the following keywords:

Stafford, Miss, Daughter, Typist, London.

The first result produced:

Elizabeth Mary Stafford, 28, Boarder, Shorthand Typist, Local Gvt Board.

Even I laughed at that! Could it be her? I decided to explore her tree.

In 1911, Elizabeth (b.1882) was living as a boarder with Maria Marsh (b.1846), a widow. Other boarders included Maria's nephew, Francis Tims (b.1892), a bookkeeper, and George Hillman Stafford (b.1892), a boy clerk with the board of customs. Could he be Elizabeth's brother?

In 1901, I found Elizabeth with her family – working as a clerk, as was her sister Ethel (b.1884). Their father, Thomas Stafford (b.1850), was also a local government clerk. Her mother was Minnie née Tomson (b.1861). I couldn't find George, but there was a Guy H Stafford of the same age. I checked back to the 1911 census and could see the name had been smudged and incorrectly transcribed. The brother was Guy!

Of course I still didn't know if Elizabeth was definitely the recipient of the postcard. However, the 1911 census address was in Camberwell, and I searched for possible locations for the office and found a likely candidate that was an acceptable distance to travel. In the most perfect postcard world, I would find Elizabeth married to a man with the initials GE. It wasn't to be. In 1923 I found her in a passenger list sailing from Mozambique to London. Her employment is given as civil servant.

015039

015039
1 February 1913
Douglas Hall
81 Tubbs Road
Harlesden, London
DD
When do you go to spend the weekend with Millie? What date in February is Will's B'day? I would like to send him a PC. This is a view of the old part San Remo.
HOSYOG

23 March 1913 Easter Sunday
81 Tubbs Road
Harlesden, London
DD
This is a view of the interior of the church I have been in today.
HOSAIEYOSG

30 March 1913
81 Tubbs Road
Harlesden, London
DD
I am up today and am much better. Hope you are well.
AMSAIEFYOS
Grace

As usual I began by searching for the recipient at the address in 1911, and there was no trace of a Douglas Hall. Frustrated because of my hefty investment in three cards, I decided to search for Douglas Hall + Grace + Harlesden.

The 1939 register had a Douglas Hall, born 1889, living with his wife, Grace.

I had nothing to lose, so I began Douglas's family tree. I had to keep an open mind as to whether this could be my Douglas. The family was easy to trace – I had Douglas's date of birth and knew he was a railway official.

In 1911, he lived in Tubbs Road – number 15 – and was employed as a railways bookings clerk. That's a mighty coincidence but I still had to keep an open mind. After all, the road number differed and Hall is a common name.

Douglas also appeared in various railway employment records and in 1903 was working at Watford Junction.

Douglas and Grace (b.1889) were both from Staffordshire. In 1901, they lived with their respective families and their fathers worked in pottery-related jobs. As I worked through Grace's story, there was something familiar about her address in 1901 – New Road, Armitage. I'd already found Douglas living at number 141 and Grace was two doors up at number 145.

Douglas's parents were Henry (b.1862) and Jessie née Salt (b.1862). Henry was a potter's placer. Douglas had two siblings – Louis (b.1892) and Edna (b.1902).

Grace's parents were Edward (b.1858) and Hannah Clark (b.1856) and Edward worked in a pottery factory. Later, in 1911, he was a miner. Grace had three siblings – Lillie (b.1885), Edward (b.1888) and Elsie (b.1896).

Of course, I was still unsure that I had the Douglas and Grace from the postcards.

I'd bought the postcards locally and the shop had a box full of cards with the same handwriting and surnames. Would I find them still there, waiting for me to discover the missing link? So, months after my first visit, I returned. Sure enough I found more postcards in Grace's handwriting – addressed to Douglas. However, this time I was more selective in which ones I considered. From dozens I chose three and they had these addresses:

36 Bruce Grove, Watford and 15 Tubbs Road, Harlesden and C/O Mrs Edward Clark, Armitage.

I know that if I'd chosen differently during my first visit I would have confirmed Douglas and Grace and their relationship far sooner. However, it's very pleasing to know my initial research was correct. Buying the extra cards might have been unnecessary – I could have just looked again and made a note. As with all family history research, having the proof is essential!

Who was Millie? The nearest possible match was Lillie Mary – Douglas's sister. I found her in 1939 living with their brother Edward in Staffordshire. At this time she was a postwoman and Edward was a railway guard.

Douglas and Grace married in 1914 – after Grace's wonderful trip to Europe. You can view all the postcards I bought to trace Douglas and Grace's story online and there are details about this later in the book.

What about the acronyms? I threw the challenge of solving them out to Twitter and Facebook and came up with some strange suggestions!

Coventry. Swanswell Gate.

016117

016117
1911

Miss Blackband
28 Queen Anne Street
Cavendish Square, London
Coventry 2.30pm
Just telephoned up. Freddie got a swollen neck. Will write you tonight.
Love from Ada.
I am going tomorrow.

Very often I was frustrated when I discovered a recipient was an employee at an address. However, with Miss Blackband's unusual name and with her employer being very thorough when he completed the 1911 census, I was able to locate her family – especially as I knew to look for an Ada.

Lucy was born in 1876 and her parents were Alfred (b.1845) and Harriet née Vernon (b.1843). Harriet had died in 1900, and in 1911 Alfred lived with his widowed son Fred (b.1874), daughter Jessie (b.1885), and a grandson, Frederick (b.1906), in Staffordshire. In 1891, Alfred is listed as a gamekeeper. Alfred and Harriet had at least six children: Fred, Lucy, Harriet (b.1878), Ada (b.1881), Sam (b.1883) and Jessie. In 1911, Ada was working as an assistant teacher in Coventry – which ties in with the information on the postcard. She was boarding with a couple – Willott (b.1888) and Annie Stone (b.1886). By 1939 she was still single and working as a teacher in Coventry.

Who was Freddie with the swollen neck? It's most likely to be Ada and Lucy's nephew, Frederick. Thankfully it wasn't a serious illness – in hindsight. He lived until 1983. Lucy never married and died in 1963.

Who did Lucy work for? In 1911, St Clair Thomson (b.1859) is listed as a widowed physician. His tree was very easily traced and I was able to chart his life from scholar, through to medical student, to doctor. He also appeared in several listings sailing across the Atlantic and around the world.

He was the second son of John Thomson (b.1816) and Catherine née Sinclair (b.1818). His brother, William (b.1846), was also a doctor. In one document St Clair is listed as *Sir* and it didn't take more than a moment to discover more about his career.

St Clair was a consultant laryngologist and even has a nasal speculum blade named in his honour. He was highly respected and worked with the medical elite of the time. So highly regarded was he that he was appointed as throat physician to King Edward VII and he was knighted in 1912.

St Clair was clearly committed to his work, perhaps more so because of the early death of his wife, Isabella née Vignoles, who had died in 1905 – just four years after the couple married. In 1939 he lived at Wimpole Street, London. Due to wartime damage, he relocated to Scotland where he was killed in an accident in 1943.

017131

017131
7 April 1911
Miss E Lamb
62 South Quay
Great Yarmouth
Dear Elsie
Awfully sorry the Mater, Pater and I are off to the Panto this evening. Should be pleased to see you dear when [?]. With love.
Maud.

With a postcard sent just days after the 1911 census had been created, I had high hopes for tracing Elsie. However, despite all of the house numbers either side of number 62 being recorded, I couldn't find Elsie's address. Nor could I find an Elsie Lamb that was a perfect fit.

However, in 1901, I found Elsie (b.1889) and her family at the address – which also included the details for the Brothers Arms – a pub I later discovered that had closed in 1923. Once I had Elsie's details, I returned to the 1911 census and found the family at Old Wellington Place – a completely different location. How inconvenient for the family to move so close to the time Elsie received a postcard!

Living with Elsie in 1911 was her father, Francis (b.1851). Although his marital status was listed as married, Elsie's mother, Louisa née Page (b.1853), had died in 1902. At this time, Francis was a shipwright and Elsie was a housekeeper. Also at the address were several of Elsie's siblings – by 1911, four of the 16 children had died. The occupations of those at home included shipwright, blacksmith, gas fitter and manager of a public business. One of the brothers, Cecil (b.1891), who was the blacksmith, served in the First World War in the Royal Navy. He was killed in 1914, serving on HMS *Monmouth*. The ship was sunk off the coast of Chile – with the loss of all those aboard.

In 1901, the family were at the Brothers Arms and Francis, Elsie's father, was also a shipwright. Two sisters, Alice (b.1881) and Lily (b.1886), were draper's assistants. Ten years earlier and Francis is recorded as a shipwright and licensed victualler in South Quay. Francis was the son of Daniel (b.1803) and Catherine Lamb (b.1811). In 1851, Daniel is recorded as a Greenwich pensioner and had been a HM coastguard.

Elsie's mother Louisa was the daughter of John Page, a sailor. At the time of Louisa and Francis's marriage in 1872, Francis was a shipwright. His father is listed as a pensioner.

What happened to Elsie? Later in 1911, she married Charles Swanston (b.1889). Charles was a cooper and the son of James (b.1836) and Agnes née Brett (b.1852). I found a possible record of their marriage in 1873 in Massachusetts and the confirmation within the 1881 census which lists one of their children, Jennie (b.1874), as being born in Massachusetts. Interestingly, their eldest child, James, was born in 1872 in Yarmouth. Had the unmarried couple left England with James and returned married with another child? It seems so.

James senior was born in Leith, Scotland. When he died in 1904 his probate records have him as a cooper and fish merchant. Agnes was the daughter of Charles (b.1809) and Mary Brett (b.1821). In 1861, Charles was an engineer in a silk factory. I found a probate record for Charles in 1871 that shows his occupation as millwright and engineer.

Until Charles's work I wasn't aware of Yarmouth's silk-making history. A website called Our Great Yarmouth has a very detailed article that tells the story of Grout & Co.'s silk factory, which traded from 1815 to 1972. During the Second World War, the company made silk parachutes.

Charles Swanston died in 1936 and his burial records confirm that he had become a fish merchant. The address given matches Elsie's in 1939.

Who was Maud? There were many single women named Maud living a short distance from Elsie and I was unable to trace her with any certainty.

Silk was imported into the UK in a raw state. It would be processed and sold on to weaving mills. By the late 1900s the industry was in decline – Female Occupations, Margaret Ward

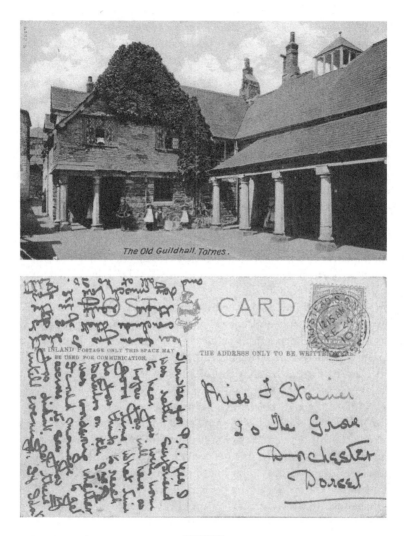

The Old Guildhall, Totnes.

018025

018025
24 Feb 1910
Miss F Stainer
20 The Grove
Dorchester
Dorset

Thanks for PC. Yes, I was rather surprised to hear you were home. Hope you will have a good time. What time do you think to reach Waterloo on the 23rd?
I was wondering whether I could manage to get across to see you if you didn't get there until evening. If I don't hear from you I shall conclude that you get there early in the day.
Much love to you and all at no 20.
Edith

The 1911 census completed by Mary Stainer (b.1859) lists all her children – even those that had died before 1911, and a son who wasn't at the address. This has all been corrected and makes for a messy document. However, it's invaluable to see all the children, irrespective of it being an error, especially as she lists two daughters named Ethel.

From that listing I began with these family members:

Mary (b.1859), Florence (b.1880), Frances (b.1884) included but deceased, Ethel May (b.1883) included but deceased, Albert (b.1886) included but not at the address, Ernest (b.1889), Ethel Louisa (b.1892), and William (b.1895).

Mary was born in Somerset and from at least 1881 lived in Dorchester. Her husband James (b.1858) died in 1898.

Ernest was a cabinet maker who married Hilda née Cross (b.1890) in 1915. William was an apprentice jeweller and then a flax worker. In 1939 he is listed as a painter and decorator.

Florence, who received the postcard, is listed as a cook in 1901. She married Edward Green (b.1883) and was living at The Grove when she died in 1918.

As I worked through the family, my tree became muddled. Ancestry had added together the neighbours – same surname – as four more children. I discovered that this new family were related to my Stainers – Herbert (b.1857) was James Stainer's brother. Other online trees had included those four people as children. Unravelling that problem was worthwhile because it revealed Edith – the sender of the postcard.

Edith Stainer (b.1883) appears in the 1891 census in Dorchester but by 1901, she is working as a servant in Braunton, Devon. The postcard was sent in 1910 from Hampstead – which suggests she left home to seek work and then moved to at least two different locations.

She doesn't appear in the English 1911 census, but is found in Canada working as a domestic servant. She had sailed from Liverpool to Canada in March 1911.

On 28 May 1914, Edith was returning to England aboard the RMS *Empress of Ireland* – a postal ship that carried 1470 passengers and crew. The captain, Henry Kendall, is famous as the captain who helped apprehend murderer Dr Crippen in 1910.

Also sailing to England from Quebec were more than 170 members of the Salvation Army, on their way to attend an international congress in London. As the ship left port, sailing down the St Lawrence River, their band entertained passengers on deck.

Albert Mullins was returning to England with his wife and daughter. Mullins and a childhood friend, Bowley Barnes, had formed Barnes & Mullins, a company that sold musical instruments. Mullins and his family had completed an international business trip and were on their way home to be reunited with their son who was at school in England.

During the early hours of 29 May the ship became cloaked in thick fog and the visibility was virtually zero. At approximately 2am the *Empress* collided with a Norwegian collier and within 14 minutes of that impact, the *Empress* sank and 1012 people lost their lives – many of them passengers.

Captain Kendall was pulled from the sea and survived. Albert Mullins and his daughter were lost. His wife survived, though with terrible injuries. All adult members of the Salvation Army lost their lives – as did Edith Stainer.

Like many people, I had not heard of this tragedy. It's often referred to as Canada's *Titanic*. In fact, more passengers were lost on the *Empress* than on *Titanic*. Why has it been largely forgotten? Some suggest that it would always be second to *Titanic*. Also, the First World War was soon to dominate the world's attention. Many of the crew were from Liverpool and, as one would expect, there are memorials there to the lost. In Canada, services of remembrance take place on the anniversary.

The Bath Postal Museum has within its archives a number of letters retrieved from the ship. They aren't always on display, but if you make a request to see them it is usually granted. When I saw them I was surprised at their good condition – hardly any indication of being water damaged. It was even possible to read the letter contained in one envelope. They had been saved during the salvage process and 318 bags of mail were brought ashore – along with 212 bars of silver bullion. The wreck remains on the bed of the St Lawrence River and is now protected.

Edith's postcard, sent before she left England, before *Titanic*, before the First World War, is such a small piece of insignificant ephemera. Yet it links to an event that hugely affected families on both sides of the Atlantic. Most of Edith's family remained close to the area around Dorchester – she paid an awful price for spreading her wings.

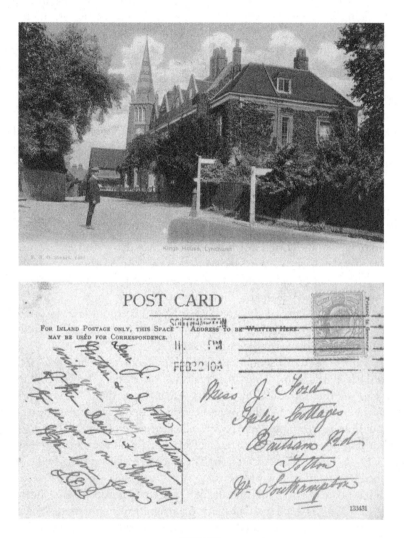

019112

019112
22 February 1910
Miss J Ford
Ipley Cottages
Bartram Road
Totton, Nr Southampton
Dear J
Mother & I both wish you many returns of the day & hope to see you on Thursday.
With love from LDD

In 1911, Jane Ford (b.1876) wasn't living at the address on the postcard. I found her as a visitor with the Wait family in Burghclere. James Wait (b.1845) was a farmer. He and his wife Sarah (b.1849) had four children and only one son was living at home at this time – Frederick (b.1880).

Jane's parents – William (b.1849) and Fanny née Flux (b.1852) – lived at the Bartram Road address. Her father was born on the Isle of Wight and he was employed in a chemical works. There were several in the area where they lived – the nearest produced wood preservation chemicals. Fanny was born in Millbrook, an area of Southampton. Jane had at least one sibling – Bessie (b.1884). By 1911, Bessie had married Herbert Saxby (b.1879), a house painter from Southampton.

In 1901, Jane – the recipient of the postcard – is listed as a boarder at another address in Burghclere and employed as an assistant teacher. She married Frederick Wait, the youngest of James and Sarah Wait's children, in December 1911. In 1939 the couple lived on a farm in Hampshire, with Jane's mother, Fanny.

Iona Cathedral

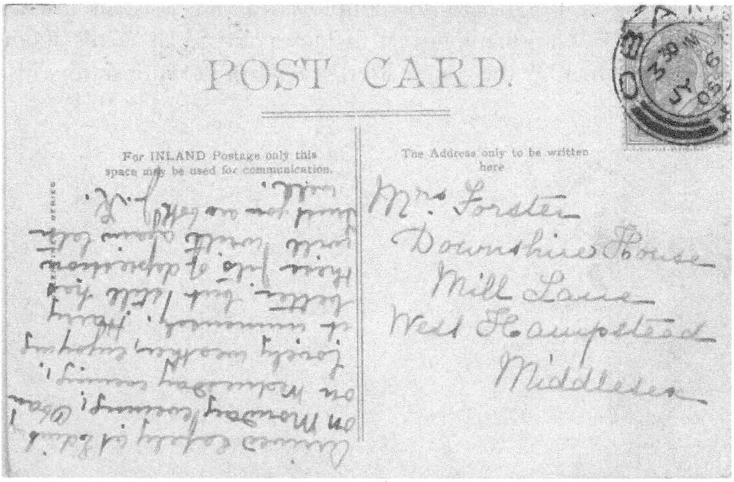

POST CARD.

For INLAND Postage only this
space may be used for communication.

The Address only to be written
here

Mrs Forster
Downshire House
Mill Lane
West Hampstead
Middlesex

020051

020051
6 July 1905
Mrs Forster
Downshire House
Mill Lane
West Hampstead
Middlesex
Arrived safely at Edinburgh on Monday evening, Oban on Wednesday evening. Lovely weather, enjoying it immensely. Harry better but still has these fits of depression. Will write again later. Trust you are both well.
JK

By the time of the 1911 census, Mrs Forster – Mary née Gayler (b.1846) had died. Living at the address was her widowed husband, Henry Forster (b.1842). Henry was born in Hampstead and was a draper. In 1901, Mary and Henry lived at the Mill Lane address with Mary's mother, Elizabeth Gayler (b.1811). In 1871, Henry was a draper's clerk and he and Mary lived with his mother, Hannah (b.1805). Hannah was a laundress and running a boarding house. According to his baptism records, Henry's father was John Forster (b.1804), a smith.

Mary Forster née Gayler, who received the postcard, was the daughter of William (b.1813) and Elizabeth Gayler (b.1811). William was a coachman. The couple had another daughter, Fanny (b.1843). In 1861, Fanny was a servant working for a widow – Mary Holford (b.1801) – and her curate son John (b.1832). In 1871, she was still a servant, this time for Charles Fox (b.1847), a law student.

In 1880 she married John Horn (b.1845), a butler working in Leigh, Surrey. In 1881, the couple lived in Leigh with four daughters: Elizabeth (b.1869), Helen (b.1871), Kate (b.1873) and Edith (b.1876) – Fanny had become stepmother to four young girls. Also staying with the couple in 1881 was Fanny's brother-in-law, Henry Forster. By 1901, John had left domestic service and become a waiter.

021074

021074
3 October 1907
Mr T Tucker Esq
North Perrott Manor
Crewkerne
Somerset
Good morning
Have you used (pears)
Bertha

I've owned this postcard for many years. I bought it for the view of Freshford. Gilbert Freeman, whose story began this book, would have recognised the buildings and the scenery. It's where he was born and lived until moving to Cornwall. The family's home, the mill, is off to the right and not in the scene. I bought it to add detail to Gilbert's story long before I had thoughts of writing this book.

Tom Tucker (b.1862) was born in Tintinhull, a small village near Yeovil in Somerset. Although I found him easily enough in 1911, working as a butler, his working career became interesting long before that census return.

His parents were Joseph (b.1819) and Mary née Russ (b.1817). Like many young women of this era, Mary was a glover. Followers of football will know from Yeovil Town FC's nickname, the Glovers, that glove-making was a prominent industry in the region. In 1871, Mary and her eldest daughters were all glovers.

In 1881, Tom appears in the census return at the 'mansion' in Montacute, Somerset as a footman. His employer was Ellen Phelips (b.1817) and her husband's family had owned Montacute House – the mansion – since the late 16th century.

Sir Edward Phelips was a successful politician who became Speaker in the first decade or so of the 17th century. His place in history was assured when he delivered the opening statement for the prosecution in the trial of Guy Fawkes and his fellow plotters. Montacute House passed into the care of the National Trust in the 20th century. The house and grounds have been used as locations in a number of films and TV programmes, most recently *Wolf Hall*.

In 1891, Tom was working as a butler, but appears in the census return living with his wife, Charlotte née Blake (b.1858), in Middle Street, North Perrott. The couple had married in 1889.

In 1901, Charlotte was in Middle Street, working as a glover. Tom was still a butler and recorded with a different employer at a different address: North Perrott Manor House – the address on the postcard. His employer at this time was the Hoskyns family who had had the house built in 1877. Henry Hoskyns (b.1822) was a magistrate and a banker. During the Second World War, pupils from a school in Surrey were evacuated to the house. Today, it's still home to children and is an independent prep school.

1911 finds Tom back at the Middle Street address with his wife, still working as a butler.

Who was Bertha? Both Tom and Charlotte came from large families and I was unable to trace a Bertha – or a branch that might lead me to Chippenham as suggested on the postcard.

According to the 1881 census, there were 5,661 glovers in England, Wales and Scotland – Tracing Your Trade & Craftsman Ancestors, Adèle Emm

BRIDGE
SEFTON PARK

POST CARD.

Write here for Island Postage only.

THE ADDRESS TO BE WRITTEN
ON THIS SIDE.

Mrs Pogson
238 Lawley Rd.
Oakes
Lindley

022079

022079
2 December 1911
Mrs Pogson
238 New Hey Road
Oakes, Lindley
Dear Sister
We hope to visit you at Christmas. Fred will write later.
I received your welcome letter safely and was surprised to hear of JR's wedding, also of Jane's death. Fred has not been well lately but kept to his work. Hoping all are well.
With kind regards
E Ramsden

Betsy Pogson née Crosland (b.1858) was a widow living at the address with her two children, Herbert (b.1893) and Clarissa (b.1906).

In 1901, the family lived at a different address in Lindley – including husband Willie Pogson (b.1866) who worked in the wool industry – as did many of their neighbours, especially as weavers. Betsy was the daughter of Jonathan (b.1821) and Ann Crosland (b.1824). In 1881, Betsy and her sister Eliza (b.1861) were weavers.

Willie Pogson was the son of John (b.1840) and Ann née Moore (b.1841). John was a stone dresser and quarryman and stone is still quarried in this area. In 1891, Willie was a cloth finisher.

In 1887, Eliza Crosland married Fred Ramsden (b.1860) and it was Eliza who sent the postcard. In 1911, Fred was a joiner, working in the construction industry. In 1871, his family lived in Dog Kennel, Almondbury. At first I thought that was a transcription error, but it seems not – it also appears in various birth records for the Ramsden children. Fred's father was George Ramsden (b.1836) and he was also a joiner. Fred's mother was Alice (b.1829).

I wasn't able to trace who had married and who died. However, Fred's illness was hopefully not too serious as he lived for a number of years after the postcard had been sent.

The Barbican, Alnwick Castle.

Mr W. Head
Brecken Hill
Brampton
Cumberland.

023089

023089
1911
Mr W Head
Brecken Hill
Brampton, Cumberland
From Mrs Douglas
Crescent Cottage
Morwick Gate
Acklington
Dearest William

I do miss those masculine arms of yours. I wish they were here to do some sowing. Never mind dear! I am coming up to see you soon, so look out for squalls. I have just had a PC from Joe. Wouldn't it be fun for you to come though on Monday. There is going to be a flower show here. We could have some dancing then.

I do wonder what the postman and William's parents thought at Mrs Douglas's message! In 1911, Thomas *William* Head (b.1889) was barely 21. He lived with parents, George (b.1851) and Elizabeth née Armstrong (b.1855), on the family farm in Brampton. The couple had five children and although the youngest, Hannah Grindley (b.1891), was married, she was at the address at the time of the census. Her husband was Robert Grindley (b.1891) and in 1911, he was living with his widowed mother, Mary née Mounsey (b.1853). Robert worked in a brewery as a brewer's assistant.

George was a farmer's son and he appears in earlier census returns working on his family's farm in the same area. George and Elizabeth's other children were Jane (b.1881), John (b.1883) and Henry (b.1887).

In 1939, John was a farmer and living with him were William (the recipient of the postcard) and his wife Hilda née Earl (b.1898), and his sister Jane. William and Hilda had married in 1929. Not all the family were farmers, Henry was a draper's assistant.

To me, the most interesting question about this card is, why did William keep it? I hope to return to Mrs Douglas another time – I'm sure there's a bigger to story to discover.

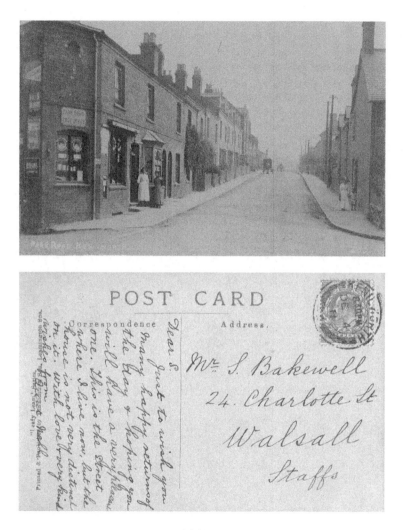

024128

MAXIM FLYING MACHINE, BLACKPOOL, TRAVELLING 40 MILES AN HOUR.

024128

70

024128
4 December 1911
Mr S Bakewell
24 Charlotte Street
Walsall
Staffs
Dear S
Just to wish you many happy returns of the day & hoping you will have a very pleasant one.
This is the street where I live now, but the house is not very distinct on it. With love & very
kind wishes from Aunt Nell.

Sidney Bakewell (b.1888) lived at the address with his father, Thomas (b.1854), a guard on a motor train, and his stepmother, Emma née James (b.1865). Also at the address was Sid's sister Marion May (b.1889). Sid is listed as a fancy leather worker and Marion was a leather purse and case preparer. Their brother Charles (b.1875), who by 1911 was married to Margaret née Astbury (b.1872), was a foreman purse maker. Thomas's first wife, the mother of the children, was Harriet née Spiers (b.1851) and she died in 1908.

Harriet had at least four siblings including two brothers – Alfred (b.1855) was a railway engine driver and Arthur (b.1860) was a bridle cutter. Their parents were Alfred Spiers (b.1832) and Charlotte née Aitken (b.1832). When the couple married in 1851, Alfred was a comb maker and Charlotte was a servant. Alfred would later work for the railways and appears in several registers as a guard. In 1901, at the age of 69, he was still working as a railway guard.

Who sent the postcard? Unfortunately a definitive Nell eluded me. There were possible sightings through the parents' siblings, but I wasn't able to prove a connection.

3 August 1907
Mr S Bakewell
C/O PSA Camp
Mr E Williams, "Tyucha"
Orme, Llandudno
Dear Sid
Just a line to say that we arrived safely & it is fine, the sea is rather rough, and there is a
nice breeze. I hope you had a pleasant journey and arrived safely. It is rather crowded, also
along the prom. Kindly drop us a card.
Yours truly George.

Who was George? He was the son of Emma Spiers (b.1862), Sidney's aunt. Emma married Solomon Roseblade (b.1862), a brush maker pan hand, in 1881, and the couple had three children, including George (b.1889). I was able to match George's handwriting on the card to his entry in the 1911 census. In later years George worked in an iron works.

What happened to Sidney, the recipient of these two postcards? He died in 1917 – killed during the First World War. His probate records confirm:

'Corporal 10th battalion Lincolnshire regiment died 3 May 1917 at Douai, France on active service'. Other military records show Sidney as a lance corporal – as does his headstone in Douai.

Despite having more than enough branches in Sidney's tree, I couldn't resist returning to the first card. The post office in Park Road, Kenilworth was easy enough to trace. In 1911 I found the Stroudley family living there.

Thirza Stroudley (b.1868) is listed as running a sub post office and store. Also at the address are her mother, Sarah née Lloyd (b.1832), and Thirza's sister, Charlotte (b.1867). Before running the post office, I found Thirza at another address as a pawnbroker. In 1901, she's listed as a pawnbroker and her mother is a rag merchant. Further back, I found Sarah's marriage to Horatio Stroudley (b.1828) and his occupation is given as rag, skin and bone merchant. Horatio's father was William Stroudley (b.1797) and his occupation was paper maker.

Could the women in the image be Thirza and Charlotte? The postcard was sent in 1906 which could have been the year the family moved to the address. It wasn't unusual for businesses to have cards printed – it was a strong market and almost a form of free advertising.

Shipton-under-Wychwood's sub-post office opened in 1847 – making it, until it closed in 1975, the oldest in the country – Post Offices, Julian Stray

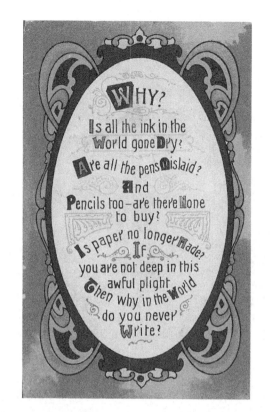

WHY?
Is all the ink in the
World gone Dry?
Are all the pens Mislaid?
And
Pencils too – are there None
to buy?
Is paper no longer Made? If
you are not deep in this
awful plight
Then why in the World
do you never
Write?

POST CARD.

"NATIONAL" SERIES.

Made in Gt. Britain
No. 1253

Correspondence

Address

So do
this as
you tells
John

Mr John Jackson
Far House
Grinleton
Nr Clitheroe

025072

73

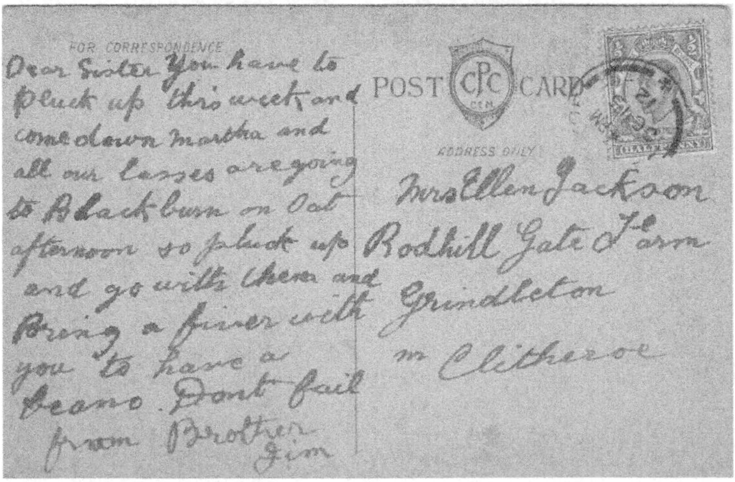

025072

1912

Mr John Jackson

Far House

Grinleton [sic]

Nr Clitheroe

So do as this tells you John.

1912

Mrs Ellen Jackson

Rodhill Gate Farm

Grindleton

Nr Clitheroe

Dear sister you have to pluck up this week and come down. Martha and all our lasses are going to Blackburn on Sat afternoon so pluck up and go with them and bring a fiver with you to have beano. Don't fail. From brother Jim.

Ellen Jackson née Smalley was born in 1863 in Clitheroe. She was the daughter of James (b.1833) and Susannah (b.1838). James was a cotton spinner and Ellen and her sisters also worked in a mill. Ellen married Stephen Jackson (b.1866) in 1889. In 1871, Stephen's father farmed 31 acres. By 1881, William Jackson (b.1841) farmed 286 acres and Stephen is listed as farmer's son – suggesting he worked on the family farm with his siblings. By 1891, Stephen and Ellen were living at the farm address on her postcard. She was still living there in 1924 when Stephen died.

The couple had five children but by 1911, one had died. The surviving children were Charles (b.1890), John (b.1893), Elizabeth (b.1894) and James (b.1898). Although I cannot confirm who sent John the postcard, the writing is very similar to his father's as shown in the 1911 census.

How do I know the cards are connected to the same family? They came from a family group and although I hate to split collections, the vendor was selling them all separately.

In 1911, John was working for James Aspin (b.1866) as a labourer on the farm at Far House. Coincidently, the neighbour was Henry Smalley (b.1844). However, I failed to fit him into this particular tree.

Because I had John's baptism records, I was able to confirm his actual date of birth and trace him in 1939 where he is listed as a bricklayer and stone-waller.

James Smalley (b.1878), who sent the other postcard, was far easier to confirm. Ellen had five siblings and the youngest was James. James married Martha née Hanson (b.1878) in 1898 and at that time both are recorded as weavers. The most recent record of the couple is in 1939, still working as weavers.

C.31879. BARMOUTH, FROM THE ISLAND.

POST CARD

THIS SPACE FOR COMMUNICATION   ADDRESS ONLY

Dear Father,
We had an hour
now on this piece of water
yesterday morning &
afterwards went to
Cregennen Lakes, 1800ft
above sea level.
With love to all
Your affec. Son
Kenneth

Mr. S. W. Hume
19 Lordship Lane
Wood Green
London N.

026035

026035
14 August 1912
Mr SW Hume
19 Lordship Lane
Wood Green
London
Dear Father
We had an hour's row on this piece of water yesterday morning and afterwards went to
Cregennan Lakes, 1800 feet above sea level.
With love to all.
Your affectionate son, Kenneth

In 1911, Sydney Hume (b.1855) was a stone lithographer and he worked in that industry from at least 1881. The card had been sent by his son Joseph *Kenneth* (b.1892) and in 1939 he was a clerk in an oil works.

Sydney's father was a brewery manager and one of his brothers, Ernest Hume (b.1859), married Elizabeth née Hofsommer (b.1862) the daughter of a licensed victualler from Germany who had moved to England in 1839. When Frederick Hofsommer (b.1815) died in 1877 he was the licensee for the Prince of Hesse in Fieldgate Street, London. Before that, in 1871, he and his family lived in the pub attached to the original Garrick Theatre in Leman Street, London.

In 1913 Ernest and Elizabeth Hume sailed to Canada with their five children. They sailed on the *Empress of Britain*, the sister ship to the *Empress of Ireland*. On the *Britain* were a high number of Salvation Army soldiers and officers – this was a period when the Army was reaching out to new communities. Would any of those be lost on the *Ireland* a year later?

Ernest and Elizabeth's youngest son, Joseph (b.1897), enlisted in the Canadian Army on 23 February 1916. He was killed a day after his 21st birthday in October 1918 and his grave is in France.

Many of the trees created in this book are directly affected by the First World War. However, this family's story goes beyond sadness. Joseph's maternal grandfather was German and when he died, Joseph's grandmother married a German widower, Jacob Genze, who became landlord of the Prince of Hesse.

The postcards included in this book were selected at random and I was surprised how many stories included travelling to Canada. In Dave Adams's book *Silverdale and Chesterton in Old Photographs*, I found a clue to the reason.

A 1904 photograph of Chesterton's post office shows a large window crammed with at least 10 posters advertising emigration to Canada. The caption suggests that emigration was actively promoted to solve the increasing numbers of unemployed workers after the boom years of the 19th century.

A website titled Canadian Immigration – Early 1900s states: In 1902 the greatest influx of immigrants in Canada's history began and continued until the beginning of World War 1 in 1914.

Another site, English Emigration to Canada 1900-1914, says that 3.15 million people left England for Canada between 1903 and 1913. That site was particularly interesting to me as it includes an image of passengers sailing to Canada aboard the *Empress of Britain* in 1911.

The Garrick Theatre opened in 1831 and closed in about 1881. The site was redeveloped and became a police station in 1891 – Wikipedia

BURLINGTON ROAD, BARRACK CORNER, IPSWICH.

027040

027040
31 January 1910
Miss King
Messel Villa
Chiseldon
Wilts
Dear Rosie
Hope you will have a very Happy Birthday. Come and see us if time. Lots of love to you and Freddie.
From Bessie

This story is a lovely example of searching for a person who might fall between the census dates.

I began with the family living at the address in 1911: Frederick King (b.1869) a baker, Elvira née Wright (b.1877), and their son Frederick Baden King (b.1909). I knew from the census return that the couple had three children and that one had died – and I later discovered him to be William King (b.1897) who had died in 1904.

Frederick was the son of a labourer. In 1881, he appears with his family aged 11 working as a labourer. His parents were William (b.1823) and Louisa née Baden (b.1832) and they married in 1852.

Elvira née Wright was the daughter of a switchman.

The card suggested that the recipient's birthday was either at the very end of January or on 1 February.

I searched for a birth of a girl after the 1901 census in Wiltshire. I discovered a Rosanna Elvira King was born in the first quarter of 1904 and registered in Swindon. As Elvira was the first name of the wife of the household in 1911, I was sure this was the recipient of the card who would have received the postcard for her sixth birthday.

Where was she in 1911? I found her living with her uncle and aunt – William (b.1839) and Rosanna Gilbert (b.1854).

Elvira died in 1912 and three years later Frederick married his second wife, Eva Mary Clifford née Webb (b.1884), a spinster dressmaker. In 1939 the couple lived with their two sons: an assistant oxy-acetylene cutter and an apprentice electrical engineer.

Who was Bessie? I know from the card that she lived nearby – but was she a relative? The choice of card seems strange – an image of a museum in Ipswich – for any birthday, let alone that of a very young girl.

Stourton Tower.

POST CARD.
Publ. by R. Wilkinson & Cᵒ., Trowbridge.

THIS SPACE AS WELL AS THE BACK MAY BE
USED FOR INLAND COMMUNICATION.
POST-OFFICE REGULATION.

THE ADDRESS ONLY TO BE WRITTEN HERE.

Mᵣ C. Coats.
The Tabernacle
Blandford
Dorset

028129

028129
15 April 1905
Mr C Coats
The Tabernacle
Blandford
Dorset

Am going to EO tomorrow if fine. Shall get there about 12. How is the knee, I do hope 'tis better. Mrs M not yet returned, could not at first understand letters, but think I know now. I don't think it would be very comfortable sitting on a bridge for 4 ? (ahem) do you? Tata etc.

In 1911, Charles (b.1853) and Emily née Hunt (b.1852) lived at the address with their son Charles (b.1879). The family were hay dealers and lived at the address through several census periods.

Emily was the daughter of Cornelius and Elizabeth Hunt (b.1830), farmers from East Orchard, near Shaftesbury, Dorset – the EO mentioned in the card's message. Who were they visiting? In 1901, I found Elizabeth and a daughter Rose (b.1861) living in East Orchard. Unfortunately the card wasn't signed and I was unable to confirm who might have sent it – surely a cousin of Charles.

Charles junior married Mabel née Arscott (b.1882) in 1912. Mabel was the daughter of Walter (b.1857) and Elizabeth née Wareham (b.1858). Mabel's baptism records show that William was a grocer. The family had a business in Salisbury Street in Blandford. Walter's probate records from 1907 confirm he was still a grocer – as was his son, Leonard (b.1882). In the 1911 census, Leonard was a manager, living with his mother and siblings – some of whom were also working in the family business, although Ronald (b.1887) and Reginald (b.1893) were draper's assistants. The 1895 *Kelly's Directory* for Blandford lists a business as Wareham & Arscott in Salisbury Street.

029123

029123
Tom Lambe
Wenny House
Chatteris
Cambridgeshire
Dear Tom
I got home but I was sick on the train.
Kathie.

In 1911, Tom (b.1902) lived with his uncle and aunt – Edward Lambe (b.1865) and Helen née Curtis (b.1865). Edward was the eldest of the Lambe siblings that I traced and was a farmer.

Tom's parents were John (b.1867) and Ethelreda née Warth (b.1874). John was a horse dealer and in 1911, they also lived in Chatteris. They had two more children: John (b.1905) and Constance (b.1910).

John had at least 10 siblings. Their parents were Edward (b.1817) and Elizabeth née Triplow (b.1841). Edward was a farmer and his brother James was a draper. Many of Edward and Elizabeth's children had connections with the drapery business. Before emigrating to Canada, Robert (b.1870) was also a draper and so were his brothers, Frederick (b.1874) and Stanley (b.1877). Another brother, Alfred (b.1872), was a window dresser.

Tom's mother, Ethelreda, was the daughter of a farmer – William (b.1816) and Amy Warth (b.1833).

Helen née Curtis had at least two siblings. Her parents were James (b.1843) and Charlotte (b.1841) from Portsmouth, Hampshire. James was a cattle salesman, as was a son, James (b.1867).

In later years, Edward Lambe lived in an almshouse in Fulham. His probate records from 1940 mention Stanley – as a draper. Helen had died two years earlier and at that time she was also living at the Fulham almshouse.

What became of young Tom? In 1927 he married Margaret née Bell (b.1907). Margaret's parents were Norman (b.1879) and Mary née Cowan (b.1879). Norman was a chauffeur, and the census return for 1881 shows that his father, William Bell (b.1850), was a butler in Ealing. Tom and Margaret's marriage register shows that Tom was employed as a draper.

At a time when most people either made their own clothes or had them made, it's not surprising that drapers – in this story and others – play such a large role in employment.

Who was Kathie? Both of Tom's parents came from large families and despite attempting to follow his aunts and uncles to trace a cousin, I was unable to do so. Of course, Kathie may not have been a relative, just a friend.

STREATHAM COMMON, SOUTH SIDE.

POST CARD

Miss G. Thompson

Chellington

Sharnbrook

Beds

030102

030102
1911
Miss G Thompson
Chellington
Sharnbook
Beds.

Thank you for the post card you sent last week. We were very pleased to get your dear mother's letter, please thank her for it. If there are any beans in the garden, be sure to gather them as it would be a pity for them to spoil. We are still having a lovely time. My boil is dreadfully painful still but I hope it is going on alright. With fond love to you all from us here. Yours affect. [?] Chandler

In 1911, Georgina Thompson (b.1895) lived with her parents, William (b.1872) and Catherine née Eyles (b.1871), her sister Daisy (b.1904) and her grandmother Susan Eyles née Isitt (b.1841). William was an electrical engineer. Catherine's father was Hugh Eyles (b.1826) and he was a carpenter.

When Susan Isitt and Hugh married in 1860, Hugh's status was a widower. Susan was a servant. The next entry in the marriage register showed the details for Sarah Isitt – Susan's sister. The sisters married on the same day. Sarah's husband was Thomas Thomson, a soldier.

Who sent the postcard to Georgina? I had a hunch it could be from someone that lived relatively nearby. I walked down the street and found Mary Chandler (b.1839). As the head of the household she had completed the 1911 census and the handwriting was a perfect match to the card.

Mary née Smith married George Chandler (b.1836) in 1862. They had seven children and by 1911 two had died. George was a Baptist minister. Through most of the census dates the family lived in Thurleigh, Bedfordshire. In 1891, their daughter Sarah (b.1863) was a schoolmistress. Ten years later and her siblings, Mary (b.1867), Chrissie – Harriet Christianna – (b.1871) and Elizabeth (b.1876) were all teachers. In 1911, Mary, Chrissie and Sarah were living together and still teaching. Mary and Sarah were head teachers. Elizabeth was unemployed and living with her mother. I traced one son to Mary and George. John Chandler (b.1868) lived in Wandsworth in 1911, and his occupation was assistant editor of 'badminton magazine' – possibly *The Badminton Magazine of Sports and Pastimes*. In 1939 he was a retired book publisher.

Finding the sender of the postcard was particularly satisfying – especially when she wasn't a relative. Of course, had she not been head of the household I could not have proven her identity.

PIER & BOWLING GREEN,
TEIGNMOUTH

THE MILTON POST CARD.

BRITISH THROUGHOUT.

FOR COMMUNICATION THIS SPACE
MAY BE USED.

THE ADDRESS ONLY TO BE
WRITTEN HERE.

The Milton. "ARTLETTE" Series No. 664. Woolstone Bros., London, E.C.

Dear Violet,

Una & Auntie are here
I wish you were here too.
We are going to Adadolon
this afternoon. With love
to all from Nora.
I am writing a letter to
mother tomorrow

Mrs. Violet French.
4 Queen St
Bude

031082

87

3 Exe Bridge
Exeter

Dear Violet
I hope you will have
a very happy birth-
day, and that you
will get a great
many presents.
I am going to break
up from school to-
morrow morning, for
seven or eight weeks.
I hope to see you in
the summer, with
lots of love from x x
x x x x Dorothy
x x x x x x x

Miss. V. French
Police Station

St Columb Minor

Cornwall

031082

031082
1910
Police Station
St Columb Minor
Cornwall
Dear Violet
I hope you will have a very happy birthday and that you will get a great many presents. I am going to break up from school tomorrow morning for seven or eight weeks. Hope to see you in the summer, with lots of love from Dorothy.

1916
4 Queen Street
Bude
Dear Violet
Una and Auntie are here. I wish you were as well. We are going to Shaldon this afternoon. With love to all from Vera. I am writing a letter to mother tomorrow.

I found Violet French (b.1903) living with her parents, Charles (b.1875) and Alice née Came (b.1874). Also at home were three other children: Alice (b.1896) – a knitting machinist, Charles (b.1898), and Eleanor (b.1900). Unsurprisingly, Charles French was a police constable.

The card sent in 1916 is signed from Vera – Alice *Vera* French.

Violet's brother, Charles, appeared in several searches (from other trees) that indicated he had served in the First World War. Before I could accept this information I needed to make sure it was the correct Charles. I had his date of birth – and had confirmed it from the 1939 register. One of the military documents gave his address at a police station and another recorded his occupation before enlisting as a watchmaker and jeweller. This tallied with the 1939 register. Charles ran a shop for a number of years and there are photos and ephemera associated with the business online. In 1939 Charles lived in Queen Street, Bude – albeit at a different number to that on Violet's second card.

Charles senior's parents were William (b.1845) and Eleanor née Mortimore (b.1842). William was a signalman with the Great Western Railway. Eleanor's father, Charles Mortimore (b.1814), was a grocer in Exeter. Alice Came, Violet's mother, was the daughter of Thomas (b.1830) and Ellen (b.1839). Thomas was a mariner.

In 1939 Violet was living with her widowed father in Teignmouth. He is listed as a retired police constable.

032042

032042
25 August 1910
Mrs G Randall
Old Basing
Basingstoke
Hants
With love from Ethel.
Having a lovely time.

I found Mrs Randall living in Old Basing. George James Randall (b.1864) was a shopkeeper and the family lived at Byfleet Stores. The family included Kate née Fyson (b.1857) and their children, Ethel (b.1889) an assistant schoolmistress, Blanche (b.1891) a telephonist, Douglas (b.1894) a clerk (although by the time of George's death in 1928 he had become a farmer) and Dorothy (b.1896).

In 1891 and 1901, George Randall was a grocer and coal merchant. In 1881, I found a George Randall working as a grocer's assistant in Bray, Berkshire. The employer was John Budgen (b.1847) – a familiar name in the grocery business, and whose family opened their first store in 1872, making it, so their website states, possibly the oldest supermarket brand in the country.

The place of birth for this George made me query if he could be my George: Park Corner, Berkshire. In other records, when with the family, his place of birth was Bisham, Berkshire. I searched for the rest of the family in 1881 without much success and decided to explore the George I'd found in 1881 – perhaps trace him and either confirm him as mine or ignore him. How many Georges were born in Berkshire in 1864–1866? Three:

George Randall, Windsor.

George H Randall, Oxford.

George James Randall, Cookham – that agreed with the full name in 1911.

Park Corner is an area in Windsor – although I was reluctant to accept the information on that basis alone.

In 1881, I found my George's parents, Francis (b.1826) and Mary (b.1825) Randall, living with George's grandmother, Frances (b.1797), in Park Corner. Next door lived another family by the name of Randall – George's eldest brother Henry (b.1853) and his wife, Catherine (b.1855).

So, I could link my George with Park Corner – and if I hadn't searched for those births and found the Cookham *and* Windsor births, I might have made the mistake of making it all fit. Perhaps they were distant cousins – I could, if I chose, track the Budgen George properly, but it would still only confirm him, possibly, as a cousin.

I returned to researching the family in Old Basing and a member of a local Facebook group kindly sent some information that wasn't available online. Anne Pitcher had a written a book *Old Basing* and it contained memories of the Randalls and their children – who were 'brought up to respect their parents, their school, and their church'. The book also mentions that Douglas served in the First World War as a farrier. Finally, the book said that George was a 'grocer by trade'. Irrespective of the possible connection with the Budgen business, it does seem that George Randall's generation was definitely associated with grocery and grocers.

In 1851 there were almost 86,000 grocers. Twenty years later the number had increased to more than 111,000 – Tracing Your Trade & Craftsman Ancestors, Adèle Emm

033127
11 August 1905
Miss MM Gandy
C/O Mr Bradburn
Chetwode Arms
Whitley
Nr Northwich
Cheshire
Grasmere Church in which is a tablet & bust to Wordsworth. The Rushbearing ceremony was to have been held when we were there but was potoned [sic] on account of weather. Hope you don't over yourself with Bacon.
Allen

Miss Gandy wasn't at the Chetwode Arms for the 1911 census – but she and Allen were found with their family in Warrington.

Mary Gandy (b.1887) lived with her parents, Henry (b.1861) and Elizabeth née Allen (b.1863), and siblings Elizabeth (b.1886), Henry *Allen* (b.1889) and Edith (b.1891). Henry senior was a house painter and plumber. Both Elizabeth and Mary were schoolteachers and Allen was a plumber. I found Mary in 1939 still working as a teacher. By this time, Allen was a master plumber. He had served in the Royal Medical Corps during the First World War.

Henry's father was Thomas Gandy (b.1824), a mechanic working in a mill. In 1871, the family lived in Warrington. Henry's mother, Elizabeth (b.1826), also worked in a mill. Two brothers, William (b.1850) and John (b.1852), were a clogger and a mechanic, respectively. Three other siblings became a teacher, grocer's clerk and milliner. By 1901, Thomas was a widower and retired engine fitter.

Mary's mother, Elizabeth née Allen (b.1863), was the daughter of a plumber and glazier, Thomas Allen (b.1828). Two of her brothers, John (b.1865) and Elias (b.1867), were also plumbers. Her mother, Eliza née Darlington (b.1838), was a confectioner and in 1881, Elizabeth was also listed as a confectioner with two siblings, Jane (b.1861) and Thomas (b.1868).

Who was Mr Bradburn of the Chetwode Arms? In 1911, David Bradburn (b.1843) is listed at the address as a farmer and hotel keeper. His wife, Sarah née Rutter (b.1839), had died in 1890 and the Chetwode had passed to David Bradburn from her family. Her own father, John Rutter (b.1805), had received the licence from his wife, Eliza née Newton (b.1809), Sarah Rutter's mother. That seemed very strange, for the pub to remain in the family through several generations, and via the female line. I found confirmation of this in a very detailed and interesting website The History of Whitley, Cheshire. When I discover these sites, created by people with a shared love of local and social history, I always acknowledge their work and, where possible, either leave a comment or email them. Very often I don't get a response because the creator of the site has either abandoned it or changed their contact details. However, in this case I received a reply within minutes. I know how important it is when people appreciate your hard work and I was pleased to connect with this researcher. As well as information about the area, there's also a lovely photo of the building on the website – still in business today.

Why the reference to the bacon? Perhaps David Bradburn had pigs on his farm and Mary was looking forward to some home-cured bacon.

Allen's message mentions a rushbearing ceremony and this dates back to a time where rushes were collected to lay on the church floor to protect the congregation from the dirt.

034048

034048
12 December 1910
Miss Cissie Cornish
The Shop
16 Victoria Street
Taunton
Local
Dear Cis
Got home alright last night but came on to rain a little after we got home. What do you think of the weather this morning. Hope you will shake hands next time I see you.
You ought to be thankful mother would not stay last night as I know we weary you very much.
You might get me the Boys' Friend for me it is 2D this week. Of course if you can't trust me for the 2D till I see you next time, you need not get it.
I wouldn't think of troubling you.
Yours etc. Jasper

In 1911, Salome Cornish née Knight (b.1869) lived at the address with her daughter, Lily Cornish (b.1894). Salome was a widow and her husband was Henry Cornish (b.1864). He had died in 1894. He is listed in 1891 as a brick manufacturer and, according to his baptism records, so was his father – William (b.1834). Salome's father, Abraham Knight (b.1830), was a farmer and in 1881 the family lived at Butty Farm in Somerset.

According to the 1911 census, Salome had two children. Albert was born in 1893 and in 1911 he was an engineer (fitter) and staying as a boarder in Earle Street, Yeovil. Another lad, Fred Easterbrook, was also lodging at the address with the same employment. Albert would later work on combustion engine research.

Salome and Lily were still living at Victoria Street in 1939 and in Salome's probate records she was there at the time of her death in 1957. The shop has now been redeveloped.

So, who was Cissie? Was it Lily? Her middle name was Naomie and I can't accept that Lily or Naomie might become Cissie. Who was Jasper? I couldn't find a Jasper in the close family and even when I ventured further afield the only Jasper Cornish I could find was not a relative. I also looked for a Jasper Knight and drew a blank. Of course, Jasper might not be his registered first name. Looking at the extended Cornish and Knight trees I was still unable to find a fit for Jasper.

5 Haddon Terrace

To dear Doris with
love from Charlie
Uncle says you had
better bring your night
dress with you and
stay the week when you
come on wednesday.

Printed in Britain

POST CARD

ROTARY PHOTOGRAPHIC SERIES

This is a Real Photograph

The Address only to be
Written Here

Miss Doris Stilton
1 y Hewlett Rd.
Roman Rd.
Old Ford
E.

035002

035002
20 April 1916
Miss Doris Stilton
17 Hewlett Road
Roman Road, Old Bow Road
[Poplar, London]
To dear Doris with love from Charlie.
Uncle says you had better bring your nightdress with you and stay the week when you come
on Wednesday.
5 Haddon Terrace

Tracing Doris Stilton was straightforward. She was born in 1904 and in 1911 lived with her parents, John (b.1871) and Sarah née Seward (b.1873), and sister, Nellie (b.1902).

Doris's father was a motor bus driver and he was born in Buckinghamshire. Her mother was born in Wales.

Having the sender's address – and one that's written so clearly – was a real bonus. But who was Charlie? Well, I knew that he might be a cousin. However, I'm always open-minded – how many of us called friends of our parents' uncle and aunt when we were young?

I needed to find who lived at Haddon Terrace – and where exactly was it? Using the 1911 census I discovered a family in Haddon Terrace in East Barnet. George (b.1876) and Alice (b.1879) Goodship lived there with their son, Charles (b.1910). George was a solicitor's clerk and his father had been a sergeant with the Metropolitan Police. I researched Charles's mother and discovered that Alice's maiden name was Seward – and she was a sister of Sarah Stilton, Doris's mum. Alice was born in Londonderry.

Sarah and Alice Seward had two brothers: James (b.1881) and Joseph (b.1885) and they were born in Woolwich and Paddington, respectively. Their parents were John (b.1843) and Emma (b.1850). James's baptism records show that John was a sergeant in the army – which explains why the children were born in their respective locations. By the time Joseph was baptised, John had become a park keeper – also confirmed in the 1891 census.

Doris's father, John Stilton (b.1871), was a motor bus driver in 1911, but in his younger years, he was a groom – confirmed in the 1891 census. By the time of the 1939 register he was a retired bus driver living with Sarah and their daughter Nellie – who was a clerk in the Seals Dept. with the GPO (in the Civil Service).

What became of Doris? She died in 1924 at the age of 20. Her death certificate confirms she was still living in Hewlett Road and that her mother, Sarah, was present at her death. The cause of Doris's death is given as heart disease. Doris was an embroideress and Charles would become a solicitor.

036062

036062
8 August 1910
Mr C Richards
Park Farm
Carn Brea
RSC
Dear Father & Mother
Received your PPC last Friday & was glad to get it. If all is well shall go to Porthpean tomorrow & in the evening shall go to a play. Miserable weather here now can't go anywhere. Shall see Helen very likely at Porthpean as her school are going there. If you don't wish to you need not write again as you know I am alright.
John

Charles Richards (b.1855) and Loveday née Friggens (b.1856) married in 1890. They had four children, but by the time of the 1911 census one had died.

William (b.1895) worked on the family farm and would later become a dairy farmer. He served in the Royal Navy in the First World War. Arthur was born in 1898. John, who sent the postcard, was born in 1893, and in 1911 he was a student teacher. He also served in the First World War in the Royal Army Medical Corps.

After the war, John continued his career as a teacher and in 1939 he is listed as a head schoolmaster in Redruth. His address is given as the School House. His wife, Nellie née James (b.1899), was the daughter of a tin mine agent, William James (b.1857).

Dolcoath mine in Redruth was known as the 'Queen of Cornish Mines'. At 3,500 feet it was for a time the deepest mine in the world. It closed in 1921 – Wikipedia

Rock Bridge.   South Brent.

Irchele,

Dear Mary.

POST CARD

We shall

FOR INLAND POSTAGE ONLY THIS SPACE
MAY BE USED FOR COMMUNICATION.

THE ADDRESS ONLY TO BE
WRITTEN HERE

be very pleased to
accept your kind
invitation with
thanks. I shall
not be able to
stay the night
as am wanted here
in the morning. May
has a very bad cold
not able to go to school
today

With love Addie

Miss M Luckraft,
Challons Coombe,
Aveton Gifford
Kingsbridge,

037068

037068
Trehele
31 January 1911
Miss M Luckraft
Challons Coombe, Aveton Gifford
Kingsbridge
Dear Mary
We shall be very pleased to accept your kind invitation with thanks. I shall not be able to stay the night as am wanted here in the morning. May has a very bad cold and not able to go to school today.
With love
Addie.

Mary Luckraft née Haddy (b.1885) lived with her husband, John (b.1884), a farmer. The couple had married the previous spring. I'm unsure why Mary was addressed as Miss – I could find no trace of John having a sister named Mary.

Mary's mother, Jane née Northcott (b.1863), died when Mary was born. Mary lived with her grandmother, Loveday Northcott née Down (b.1834), and appears in the 1901 census with Loveday, who was a widow. I struggled to trace her husband but believe he was Richard Northcott (b.1829), a copper miner in Calstock, Cornwall and he died in 1865. I found Mary in various trade directories. She had a shop in Looe Street, Plymouth from at least 1891. Later, in 1893, her business has relocated from number 1 to number 3.

I decided to see if I could trace Addie. I had no surname and searched for an Addie living in Modbury. That didn't reveal anything conclusive, which wasn't a surprise as I assumed Addie was a shortened version of her name. So, I searched for May. Within moments I found May Luscombe (b.1905) living with her parents, Arthur (b.1866) and Lucy née Rogers (b.1867), and siblings Herbert (b.1892) and Adelaide (b.1895) at Trehele in Modbury, Devon.

The larger Luscombe family appears in several records – as farmers and innkeepers. In 1911, Addie worked in the dairy of her family's farm.

In 1881, her paternal grandparents, Aaron (b.1835) and Elizabeth (b.1841), are listed at Brownston Public House and farmer of 21 acres.

Addie's mother Lucy was the daughter of a farmer. Richard Rogers (b.1840) and Mary née Blackler farmed 71 acres. Her two brothers, Richard (b.1862) and Philip (b.1872), were also farmers.

Herbert became a farmer and Addie married a farmer and continued living in Devon.

Swanage Church, Dorset.

POST CARD.

THE ADDRESS ONLY MAY BE
WRITTEN HERE

Mrs Gedling
No 6 Newlands
Place
Penrith

038010

038010
Mrs Gedling
No 6 Newlands Place
Penrith
Dear A
I may be down on Tuesday but am not sure all depends if [?] can come to meet me as I will bring your butter. Tell Maggie, Jim got second at Crosby on Thurs with Bob.
Love to all
Your aff sis Lizzie.

Because the postcard's stamp had been removed, I didn't know when the card had been posted. However, I found Alice Gedling née Hullock (b.1873) at the address in 1911. Also at the address were her husband, Stephen (b.1869), and their only child, Mary (b.1896), who was a dressmaker's apprentice. Stephen was a railway porter. The couple had married in 1895 and were listed at the same address in 1901.

Alice's father was George Hullock (b.1832), a farmer. As a young man, he worked as a servant for a farmer in Cumberland. Also there at the time of the 1851 census was a lodger, William Gedling (b.1782) – a slater. Unfortunately I couldn't link this Gedling to the family of Alice's husband – but that doesn't mean there isn't a link!

In 1891, Alice is listed as living with her uncle and aunt – Robert (b.1837) and Mary Hullock (b.1854). Robert was hotel keeper of the Hullock Hotel, Station Road, Workington. The hotel was included in *Bulmer's Directory of 1901* (found via an online transcription) as the County Temperance Hotel – run by Mrs MA Hullock. In 2015, plans were lodged to covert the building and the neighbouring property into accommodation for adults with either learning or physical disabilities.

Alice (who received the card) had at least seven siblings. The postcard was most likely sent by Elizabeth (b.1865), and in 1881 she worked as a servant for a farmer of 500 acres, Richard Richardson (b.1846), in Brougham. Ten years later, she was back at home, presumably helping on the family farm. Who was Maggie? Probably Alice and Elizabeth's sister Margaret (b.1871). The eldest sibling was James (b.1860) – who also worked on the family farm.

I found Alice and Stephen in 1939 still living at Newlands Place and both were at that address at the time of their deaths (Stephen in 1949 and Alice in 1960). Alice had lived in Newlands Place for at least 60 years.

Clarence Park, Weston-super-Mare.

POST P.H./W. CARD

ADDRESS ONLY

Dear A.
Just a line hoping
you are all quite well, as
it leaves me at present,
are you coming down
before Xmas. If so bring
the children, or as they
can the father Xmas
in the walks about the street,
much love to all from B.B.

Mrs A. Willmott
Horsecastle
Yatton
Som.

039047

106

039047
10 December 1912
Mrs A Willmott
Horsecastle
Yatton
Somerset
Dear A

Just a line hoping you are all quite well, as it leaves me at present. Are you coming down before Xmas. If so bring the children, so as they can see Father Xmas. He walks about the streets much love to all from BB.

In 1911, Alice Willmott (b.1877) lived with her husband Jacob (b.1880), their son Jack (b.1901) and their two daughters, Gladys (b.1902) and Emily (b.1907).

Jacob's employment with the railways began in 1898 as a porter in Chippenham. He is listed later as being a goods shunter and more latterly as a ticket collector with Great Western Railway. In August 1911, he was commended for his prompt action in an emergency on 19 May 1911. The couple had married in 1901.

In 1891, Alice née Beacham – then only 13 – worked as a domestic servant for Charles Stuckly – a farmer. Her father was Joseph Beacham (b.1840) a labourer. Her mother was Mary née Drissell (b.1844). In 1861, Mary worked as a servant for the Burdge family in Yatton.

Who was BB? Could he be William (Bill) Beacham (b.1862) – Alice's brother? In 1911, he lived with his mother Mary. His daughter, Elizabeth (b.1895), could have been Bessie – she is listed as Bessie in 1901.

040058

040058
24 December 1908
Mrs Emerson
45 Earl Street
Grimsby
Dear Jennie
Wishing you and Fred a happy Xmas love from Mother.

In 1911, Jennie Emerson née Hale (b.1879) lived with her husband, Wilfred (b.1853), in Earl Street. They had a son, Wilfred, who was born in 1903. It seemed strange that Jennie's mother didn't wish her grandson a happy Christmas – but maybe she considered the child was too young to be included. Wilfred was a painter and house decorator and Wilfred junior would follow his father's trade.

The card was sent by Jennie's mother, Mary Hale née Turner (b.1856). Mary had at least six siblings and one brother was named George Turner (b.1863). Her father, George Turner (b.1834), was an engineer, working on a steam tug. Later, he is recorded as a marine engineer.

Jennie was born in Grimsby and her father, William Hale (b.1853), was a ship's carpenter from Essex. She had two siblings: Byron (b.1883) and Eveline (b.1888).

By 1871, the family had moved from Essex to Lincolnshire where William was an apprentice carpenter. He would eventually work as a shipwright. In 1939 Byron lived next door to his parents.

What took the family to Lincolnshire? William's father, also William (b.1824), was involved in the fishing industry. A Barking trade directory from 1862 lists William Hale as a smack [small fishing boat] owner. During the 1860s the fishing trade was waning and smack owners were relocating to places such as Grimsby. In 1871, he was master of *Gem,* a 32-tonne smack, fishing off Well Bank, Grimsby with a crew of five, including a cook. Finding a vessel in a census return was a lovely bonus – especially as it included the boat's size.

Stone Bridge on Mechanic Street
Attleboro, Mass.

POST CARD

Dear Harry
    Just a card to let
you know everything
is over its a boy
Nance says the parcel
has arrived with a
tassel on 10-40 Tuesday
night   with love
            Harold

Mr H Standrin
No 3 Victoria cottages
Occupation Road
Wormley
Nr Broxbourne

041060

041060
19 April 1911
Mr H Standrin
No. 3 Victoria Cottages
[?] Road
Wormley
Hertfordshire
Dear Harry
Just a card to let you know everything is over [and] it's a boy. Nance says the parcel has arrived with a tassel on 10.40 Tuesday night.
With love
Harold

I began by searching for two siblings – Harry and Harold Standrin. It was clear that the card wasn't sent from one friend to another. But would two brothers share a very similar name? It seems so.

Harry was born in 1884 and Harold in 1889. They also had a sister, Martha (b.1891).

In 1911, Harry was living at the address on the card with his wife, Elsie (b.1887). They had been married one year and had no children. Harry was a nurseryman.

At the same time, Harold was living in St Albans with his father, Benjamin (b.1854), his wife, Annie née Vass, and his sister, Martha (b.1891). Harold was a tailor cutter. Harold and Martha had married just before the 1911 census.

According to the postmark, Harold had written to his brother on 19 April – announcing the safe arrival of the baby. Benjamin Standrin was born on 18 April.

Harold and Annie would have other children – at least three more sons, and they would all marry and have families of their own.

What happened to young Benjamin? He died in 1918 and his death certificate records that he had suffered from pneumonia for several weeks.

Lynton. Hunters Inn

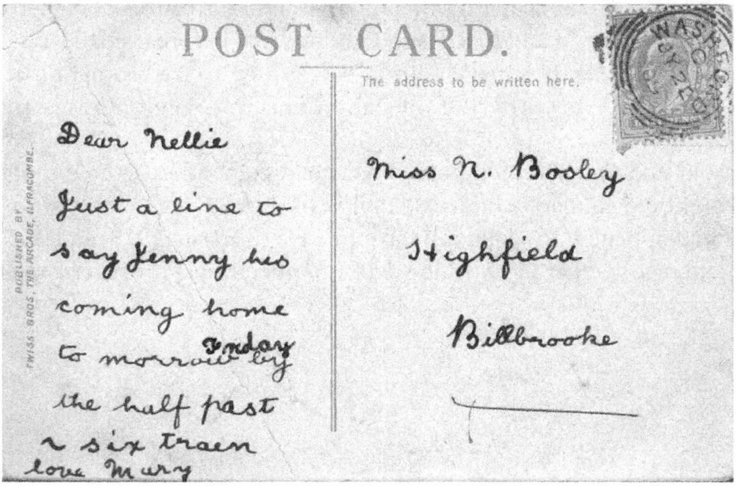

POST CARD.

The address to be written here.

Dear Nellie

Just a line to
say Jenny has
coming home
to morrow by Friday
the half past
a six traen
love Mary

PUBLISHED BY
TWISS BROS THE ARCADE, ILFRACOMBE.

Miss N. Booley

Highfield

Bilbrooke

042037

042037
22 July 1909
Miss N Bosley
Highfield, Billbrook
Dear Nellie
Just a line to say Jenny was coming home to morrow Friday by the half past six train.
Love Mary

This postcard is another of those addressed to someone with a pet name – there is no Nellie in the Bosley family tree. Fortunately, Nellie was at the address in 1911, and I was able to confirm her identity as Ellen Bosley (b.1891), born in Nettlecombe, Somerset. Nellie was employed by a retired farmer and his wife – John (b.1842) and Emma Hill née Button (b.1843).

In 1901, Nellie lived with her family – parents James (b.1851) and Elizabeth née Langdon (b.1857). James was an agricultural labourer. Both parents were born in Old Cleve, Somerset.

From the parents' listing in 1911, I knew that Nellie had nine siblings. At that time, and in 1901, the family lived in Egypt Cottages, Nettlecombe.

Laura (b.1881) married Ambrose Hayward (b.1881), a plumber. In 1911, the couple lived in Taunton. Before she married, Laura worked as a domestic nurse for a pawnbroker and jeweller.

Edmund (b.1883) married Winifred née Lea (b.1880) and was a house painter. In 1911, they lived in Victoria Terrace, Alcombe. The terrace has been absorbed into a larger road that leads into Minehead, but the distinctive brickwork makes it very easy to locate the terrace. The couple were still at the address in 1939.

Arthur (b.1885) died in 1935 and his probate records shows his place of death as Alcombe Brickyards. Approximately 24 men were employed at the site at this time.

Charles (b.1887) was a gardener and in 1911 he was living in Carhampton with his wife, Elizabeth née Squance (b.1886). In 1901, at the age of 14, Charles worked as a page boy in Treborough Lodge, Roadwater. His duties would have included running errands and generally helping within the household. Emma (b.1889) married Alfred Bees (b.1882), a plumber. Eva (b.1896) married Robert Eaton (b.1893), a chauffeur. In 1939, he is registered as an air raid warden. In 1939, Nora (b.1898) was unmarried and living in Minehead as a maid. Stanley (b.1901) died in 1911, just after the census date.

At the time she sent the postcard, Mary (b.1894) was a nursemaid at Parsonage Farm, Watchet. Her employers were John (b.1880) and Marjorie (b.1886) Stoat.

Nellie married William Milton (b.1887), a painter and decorator.

Who was Jenny? I can only believe that Jenny was a pet name – I couldn't find a Jenny in the immediate tree.

PORT SAID - Rua arabe

A. Mc Fill
8 Mansfield Terrace
Alfreton
Derbyshire

043093

043093
M Till
8 Mansfield Terrace
Alfreton
Derbyshire

Although this postcard was never sent, I still thought it might be worth researching. In 1911, I found Dorothy Till (b.1910) living at Mansfield Terrace with her parents, Arthur (b.1885) and Ada née Fowkes (b.1888). The head of the household was Ada's father John Fowkes (b.1863). Also in the home was Ada's mother, Mary née Goodacre (b.1844). Despite John being head of the household, it was his daughter Ada who completed the return.

Arthur was born in Leicestershire and was a miner. At the time of Dorothy's baptism in 1910, the family's address is given as 7 Mansfield Terrace – one number away from the address on the postcard. Arthur Till was also a miner.

In 1891, John Fowkes was a brickyard labourer and the family lived in Leicestershire – where John, Mary and Ada were born. In 1891, John's father, William (b.1833), also worked in a brickyard, as did John's brother, Frederick (b.1874).

In 1901, John, Mary and Ada were living with Frederick and his wife, Sarah (b.1877), and their family. At this time Frederick was a brick and terracotta maker.

Mary was the daughter of Samuel (b.1822) and Ann Goodacre (b.1817) and she worked as a dairymaid on the family farm.

Dorothy married John Johnson (b.1903), a coalminer. I imagine, although it cannot be proven, that Dorothy wrote the card. If you look carefully, you can see that whoever did write the card has practised their letters on the top edge, using pencil. Using pencils was clearly a family trait – the census entry had also been written in pencil before the details were inked in by Ada.

CONISTON LAKE FROM FIR ISLAND.

POST CARD.

THIS SPACE CAN BE USED FOR INLAND
CORRESPONDENCE ONLY.

THE ADDRESS ONLY TO BE
WRITTEN HERE.

Dear Uncle & Aunt
—Just a line to tell you that I have
passed my exam: which I
sat for before Christmas. Papa
all are well. With love,
Ivy.

Meadow House
Spring Vale
Cwmra
Feb. 15th 09

M.rs J. Rudd
No. 16 High St
Killamarsh
N.r Sheffield

044109

116

044109
15 February 1907
Mrs J Rudd
No. 16 High Street, Killamarsh
Nr Sheffield
Meadow House
Spring Vale, Clowne
Dear Uncle & Aunt
Just a line to tell you that I have passed my exam which I sat for before Christmas. Hope you are well.
With love.
MJ

When I read the message on this card I assumed I'd be tracing the sender – perhaps discovering what exams they may have passed. However, I was led on a different journey that took me to the heart of industrial Britain.

In 1911, I found Mary Rudd née Moseley (b.1848) living as a widow with her mother, Mary (b.1823). Mary's husband was John Rudd (b.1849) and he had died in 1909. Of course, I wanted to know who had written to their uncle and aunt and I began creating the family's tree.

John and Mary's daughter Elizabeth was born in 1866 and that suggested that I was looking for someone who might have been either a great-nephew or great-niece.

I found it difficult to follow the correct siblings of John and Mary Rudd – especially those that might lead me to the niece or nephew. Usually I have been able to begin a search in the 20th century and work back, but with this family I was working in the mid-1800s and it's difficult to achieve accurate success by only using online resources. As I've mentioned elsewhere, it's never recommended that you should rely entirely on this method.

John Rudd was a boiler fireman at a coal mine. All of the men on the same census pages in 1901 worked in a mine – I suspect even the clerk in an accounts office was employed by a mine.

In 1861, John was a scholar and his father, Thomas Rudd (b.1812), was a farm bailiff. His two brothers, William (b.1835) and James (b.1840), were ploughmen.

Mary Mosely's father, George (b.1822), was also a miner. When she was only 13, Mary was a servant, working for a farmer of 64 acres.

John and Mary had one daughter – Elizabeth (b.1866). She married Hugh Hall (b.1861), a coalminer hewer (working below ground). In 1911 their sons, Charles (b.1889) and John (b.1893), also worked for a mine – as a mining filler (usually assisting a miner) and clerk, respectively. I believe that the sender of the postcard would most likely have been from the same generation as Charles and John.

What of the sender's address? That also proved difficult. Spring Vale was a row of terraced houses that appear in a depressingly titled page 'Demolished Buildings' on the Clowne Village website. Killamarsh Heritage Society has a wonderfully detailed website, celebrating and commemorating the area's industrial past.

Although I was disappointed not to trace the student, the card led me to explore Nottinghamshire and Derbyshire's mining history. Clowne, the village from where the postcard was sent, is on the border between the two counties and the extended family lived mainly in Derbyshire.

When you view the census returns from the 19th century, Britain's industrial past leaps from the pages. Families, streets, communities worked within a limited employment. In some areas it would be the mills, for this family it was the coal mines – so many relying on just one source of employment and the fragile extended economy also dependent on that income. For the families who earned their living below ground, we know how dangerous it was. Even when a man retired, ill-health would often follow with diseased lungs and damaged limbs.

My own family has roots in an industrial Britain, working in an ironworks. In the census returns of the late 19th century, my ancestors lived in a Staffordshire community where men – and children – worked in mines and ironworks. In the same street as my great-grandfather a 13-year-old lad worked in a mine, as did his father and two brothers. Another near neighbour had two boarders, a widowed father and his 13-year-old son. Both worked in a coal mine. Several of my ancestors were listed as puddlers – their role covered many tasks including tending furnaces and stirring molten iron with a long-handled bar. Perhaps it's because of my own past that I feel so connected to this particular card.

John and Mary would, I think, have been proud to read the news about the exam success. Who knows what career beckoned for that student?

The Crosses, Sandbach.

POST CARD.

FOR INLAND POSTAGE THIS SPACE MAY NOW
BE USED FOR CORRESPONDENCE.

THE ADDRESS ONLY TO BE
WRITTEN HERE.

50 Park St. Crewe

Dear Ceila

I hope to arrive
at Moreton. 8.40
tomorrow Friday
Best Love from

Your Aunty Nodu

Miss Ceila Gill
"Llansannor"
Bourton-on-the-Hill.
Moreton-in-Marsh.

045110

045110
1911

Miss Ceila Gill
Llansannor, Bourton-on-the-Hill, Moreton-in-Marsh
50 Earle Street, Crewe
Dear Ceila
I hope to arrive at Moreton 8.40 tomorrow, Friday.
Best love from your Aunty Rhoda.

In 1911, Rhoda Rollings (b.1882) lived with her brother, Harley (b.1879), in Crewe. Harley Rollings was a commercial traveller and Rhoda is listed as a greengrocer. Ten years earlier and she was living with her widowed mother, Caroline née Preece (b.1841), in Yarpole, Herefordshire – both were laundresses. James (b.1835) and Caroline Rollings had at least six children: Caroline (b.1865), Elizabeth (b.1866), Emily (b.1870), Arthur (b.1874), Harley and Rhoda. In 1871, James was a farm bailiff in Yarpole. His role would have included managing and supervising agricultural workers.

In 1901, Harley was a boarder in Toxteth, Liverpool and worked as a grocer's assistant. In 1915 he married Lily née Wilkinson. In 1923, Lily appears in a trade directory for Cheshire, listed as a confectioner. By 1939 Harley was a widower staying in a hotel in Llandudno. His employment is described as a dealer of sugar confectionery and a wholesale cheese buyer.

Rhoda and Harley's sister Elizabeth married George Rollings (b.1865) – they shared the same surname – in 1894. George was from Radnor in Wales. In 1901, he was employed by a Merthyr Tydfil colliery, working below ground. Unsurprisingly, very few men in their district worked outside of the mining industry. In 1911, their eldest son, Edwin (b.1895), worked as a haulier. George was still a miner and still below ground.

Arthur Rollings was a cheese agent in Cheshire. Ten years earlier in 1891, he was a grocer's apprentice in Shropshire. He's listed in the 1911 census with his wife of nine years, Elizabeth (b.1875), and employed as a Cheshire cheese buyer.

Who was Ceila? She was born in 1907 and her mother was Caroline – the eldest of James and Caroline Rollings' children. Caroline married Frederick Gill (b.1863), a stonemason from Gloucestershire, in 1898. I found Ceila in 1939 working as a typist in Slough. She also appeared in passenger lists, sailing from Mozambique in 1958. At that time she was living in Maidenhead and employed as a private secretary.

It seems strange that Rhoda wrote a postcard to her young niece – I was surprised when I discovered how old Ceila was at that time. Rhoda had many nephews and nieces and by 1911, two of Ceila's siblings had died – including Byron (b.1899) who died in 1906.

View from Hotel Gardens, Cheddar.

POST CARD

THE ADDRESS ONLY TO BE
WRITTEN HERE

Come & have some
cheese, duckie!!!!!
This is our last day
so we are having
a trip to the famous
Cheddar caves &
cliffs. Home, sweet
home, tomorrow!
Much Love ~ old Jvob?

Miss Riches
Harwood Villa
Norton Road
Greenway
Uxbridge

046113

121

046113
18 February 1908
Miss Riches
Harwood Villa
Norton Road
Greenway
Uxbridge
Come & have some cheese, duckie!!!!
This is our last day so we are having a trip to the famous cheddar caves & cliffs. Home,
sweet home, tomorrow!
Much love – old Food[?]

Amy Riches (b.1891) lived with her parents, Elton (b.1868) and Amy née Bolton (b.1868), in Uxbridge. Elton was a railway clerk – and had been all his working life. The earliest record I found for his employment was in 1882 when he was 14 and employed by Great Western Railway as a lad clerk.

Elton was the son of Francis Riches (b.1835), a surgeon. Elton's mother was Lucy née Goodwin (b.1839). When Francis and Lucy married in 1859, Francis is recorded as a chemist. Two years later he had become a medical assistant. He is recorded as a surgeon in his children's marriage records. Francis died in 1874 and Lucy's second husband was Robert Tow (b.1836), a bootmaker from Southwark.

Amy Bolton was the daughter of Silas Bolton (b.1819) a coach maker from Kingston in Surrey. In 1881, Amy was living with her brother James (b.1849) and his wife, Mary née Simmond (b.1849). The family lived at the Garibaldi Beer House in Iver, Buckinghamshire. James was also a wheelwright – in addition to running the beer house. The Garibaldi no longer exists – it was demolished and the site forms part of the area now developed as a village hall. Amy died in 1915. In 1921, Elton married Lily née Welsh (b.1882), the daughter of William Welsh, a clerk.

Beer houses were just that – a room in a house from which beer was served. Adèle Emm's book *Tracing Your Trade & Craftsman Ancestors* explains how the licensing of such premises in 1872 introduced closing times of 'midnight in towns and 11pm in the countryside so that workers could walk home by midnight'.

Amy Riches, who received the postcard, married Ted Smith in 1921.

047030
19 October 1910
Mrs Harrison
31 Lee Terrace
Blackheath
SE
Here is another of Oare Church for you. It's nice & fine & as soon as the post is in we are going to Oare Valley to see the church.
Love from HL

Agnes Harrison née Tupper was born in Guernsey in 1845. She had at least five siblings. In the 1851 census, she lived with her parents, Augustus (b.1805) and Margaret née Crouch (b.1824), and her siblings Lilla (b.1844), Edith (b.1847), Augusta (b.1849), Augustus (b.1850) and John (b.1853). Augustus senior was an accountant.

Agnes married Charles Harrison (b.1829) in 1872. Charles was a tea merchant. They appear in the 1881 census, living in Kent. With them were Arthur (b.1861) and Maud (b.1862) – children of Charles's first marriage. Charles's first wife was Mary née Jeffreys (b.1832) and she was born in India and the daughter of a doctor. Charles and Mary had at least 12 children and they appear in various census returns as boarders at schools in the UK. Mary died in 1870.

Agnes and Charles had three children: Mabel (b.1873), Hilda (b.1874) and Nora (b.1876). In 1910 Hilda married Frank Longstaff (b.1877) and I believe the postcard was sent by Hilda during their honeymoon. Frank was a coal merchant and in 1911, just a few months after the marriage, the couple lived with two servants in Lewisham. According to Frank's baptism records, his father, John, was also a coal merchant. The family tradition continued with Frank and Agnes's son John (b.1912) who also became a coal merchant.

LOCH KATRINE & BEN VENUE, TROSSACHS

POST CARD
DAINTY PHOTOGRAVURE SERIES

FOR CORRESPONDENCE   FOR ADDRESS

DONCASTER
10 PM
13 JUL
1939
YORKSHIRE

Kind thoughts & good wishes

10. 7. 39
P. C. received &
J. My address is :-
11 A Crossways North
Wheatley Hills
Doncaster
Yorks.

Miss Pointon
Knoll Bank
Beeston Common
Sheringham
Norfolk

048075

125

048075
Miss Pointon
Knoll Bank, Beeston Common
Sheringham
Norfolk
10 July 1939
Your PC received today. My address is:-
11A Crossways North, Wheatley Hills
Doncaster, Yorks
Kind thoughts & good wishes.

Emmeline Pointon (b.1856) was the eldest daughter of Jeremiah Pointon (b.1827) and Maria née Creamer (b.1821). Jeremiah was a master baker from Norfolk. In 1881, he appears in a trade directory as a baker and confectioner in West Riding, Yorkshire.

Emmeline was born in Field Dalling, Norfolk. In 1881, the family were living in Yorkshire and Emmeline worked as a dress and mantle maker. Her two sisters also lived in the family home – Elinor (b.1857) and Evangeline (b.1859). Their employment is recorded as baker's daughter and schoolmistress, respectively.

By 1891, Elinor was working as a shop assistant for a confectionery business, perhaps her father's.

In 1901, the family were still together in Yorkshire. Elinor's role had changed to bread-maker. Both she and Jeremiah worked at home in Back Lane, Horsforth. Much of that road has been redeveloped, but it's still possible to see small cottages, perhaps where the family baked and their customers lived.

Maria, the girls' mother, had died in 1901, and by 1911, the family had returned to Norfolk and lived in Sheringham. Emmeline was now an office manageress in a laundry. Despite Jeremiah being head of the household, Emmeline completed and signed the return. Evangeline had died by this time – but the surviving sisters were still with their father.

Elinor died in 1928 and Emmeline died not long after the postcard had been sent, in January 1940.

Although I wasn't able to discover too much about the Pointons, I do feel a great sense of family associated with them. They were together for as long as they lived. However, we shouldn't romanticise the past – three spinster sisters living with their parents cannot always have been an easy situation.

When Emmeline died she was living at an address with others of a similar age. The head of the household was an ex-nurse – who was most likely caring for the residents in some capacity.

Culdees Castle, Muthill.

049053

127

049053
April 1907
Miss Frost, 28 Wilton Place
London
This is our Highland Castle. Will write in a day or two.
Kind regards to all.
MS Hamilton

Eliza Frost (b.1876) was a housemaid, working for Jessie Head (b.1860), a widow from New South Wales, Australia. It was a relatively large household. Eliza was one of six staff, including Marion Cordukes (b.1866), a companion from Australia.

Eliza was born in Islington. That, and her approximate birth year, was all I had. Fortunately I only found one birth that seemed to fit: Elizabeth Mary Frost (b.1876). However, that didn't provide anything conclusive so I decided to look for her employer – perhaps they were together in 1901?

I began creating a tree for Jessie Head, adding her location in 1911. Although it clearly stated that she was born in New South Wales, Australia, the information had been transcribed as Wales – a cautionary tale to anyone with Welsh or Australian ancestry! That carried through to the 1901 census where the same error had been made. Eliza didn't appear with her – in Caxton Street, Westminster. However, Jessie's sister, Mary Florence Lynch (b.1857), is listed as being born in London and was a widow. As Mary had been born in the UK I knew I'd have more success tracing her than her sister. In 1911, she is listed at the Ladies' Park Club, Knightsbridge.

Without knowing Mary's maiden name, there was little I could find. So, I searched for births around 1857 for a Mary Florence and I found Mary Florence McLean. This matched a marriage in 1876 in Kensington to William Wiltshire Lynch (b.1831).

So, Jessie and Mary's maiden name was McLean.

A search took me to the newspaper *Belfast News Letter* where I found the announcement of Mary and William's marriage. It also told me that she was the daughter of the late JD McLean (b.1820) of Australia. William was born in Ireland. In the marriage records, Mary is 19 and listed as a minor. William is a lieutenant colonel (in later documents he is a major general). Both fathers are recorded as gentlemen.

By now I had the foundations to a solid tree and I explored the other trees that had been created for this branch of the family. One gave me the birthplace for the father – Snizort in Inverness-shire. Also, that the mother was Mary née Strutt (b.1839) and that she was born at sea. The couple married in Australia.

William Lynch died in Allahabad, India in 1888. A website confirmed that he had died from cholera. Mary and William had two children. Their son,

Colmar William Donald Lynch DSO (b.1881), was killed in 1916 and is buried in France.

I then reverted back to Jessie and began my own searches – ignoring any information in other trees. I discovered that she had married barrister Frederick William Head (b.1854). His father was Sir Francis Somerville, 2nd Baronet Head of Rochester (b.1818). Frederick died in Cyprus in 1886.

Now I had Jessie and Mary's tree relatively resolved, I decided to look at their mother, Mary Anne Elizabeth née Strutt (b.1839). As well as marrying John McLean in 1855, I found two additional marriages – to Thomas Platt in 1872 and Robert Gandell in 1883.

By the time I had finished exploring Mary's marriages, I was able to confirm she had 10 children, including Percy who died during the voyage from Australia to England. Percy hadn't appeared in the other trees I explored but I'm happy that he should be included.

Something about the postcard itself had piqued my interest: *This is our Highland Castle*. John McLean had been born in Scotland – was there a connection with the castle? I began with the 1911 census and found the Speir family. I decided to create their tree – hoping to find a common surname. Within minutes I had traced the head of the family's marriage – Robert Speir (b.1841) and Emily née Gifford (b.1847). Life's full of coincidences, but my next discovery was a spine-tingler. Their marriage had been announced in the same Belfast newspaper as Mary and William's had.

The image on the postcard is of a grand castle. An online article by *The Scotsman* in 2017 provides the following information:

Set in the picturesque village of Muthill, in Perthshire, the B-listed castle dates from 1810 and was built for Charles Drummond, whose clan were gifted the land by Robert the Bruce after the Battle of Bannockburn.

I decided to explore William Wiltshire Lynch's family. I knew from the marriage records that his father was Samuel Smith Lynch (b.1795). The immediate searches returned lots of hits connected with Barbados. However, before I accepted any of those, I had to find William. He was born in Ireland. Could I connect Ireland and Barbados? I found a possible mother – Catherine née Cox (b.1801) also had links to the West Indies.

I then reviewed other trees that focused on Samuel Lynch as the main branch. This confirmed what I'd independently discovered about Catherine and their children. Apart from one of her children, all were born around the world – only William was born in Ireland. Both parents were born in the Caribbean. By this time, this postcard's tree had morphed into a forest. I'd found out so much about Jessie's family – where they'd lived, where they'd died. It was a shame not to connect the family with the castle – apart from the coincidence of the Belfast newspaper.

It was also a shame not to discover Eliza's story, but her postcard took me on a journey far beyond the Scottish Highlands.

050016

050016
10 October 1910
6C Lynn Street
Balham
SW
Dear Doris
Thanks for PC you sent me. I would very much like the set. Would you like the set of Pageant? I came to London with father a fortnight ago and went to the Exhibition. Kind regards to all. Yours truly H Grant

Elsa *Doris* Wilson (b.1896) lived with her parents, William (b.1870) and Fanny née Brain (b.1866), and her three sisters: Florence (b.1893), Violet (b.1900) and Ivy (b.1904).

William was a tailor's cutter and his father Henry (b.1830) was a railway porter. William's brothers' jobs included postman, Tube attendant and telegraph messenger.

In 1911, Florence was a milliner's assistant. In 1939 Doris and Florence are shown at the same address in Leatherhead. Doris was employed as a clerical officer, civil servant. Violet was employed as a model gown hand dressmaker, living in Wandsworth. Ivy was a dispenser bookkeeper, living in Chelmsford with Fanny.

I wondered if it might be possible to trace H Grant. All I knew was that he lived in Oxford and I assumed he must be around the same age as Doris. Surprisingly, I was able to find a very short list of candidates.

I decided that the most likely person was Harold George Grant (b.1900). In 1911, he lived with parents, George (b.1861) and Emma (b.1861), and two brothers, Arthur (b.1892) and Percy (b.1894).

George was a builder's manager with the Co-op Society, Arthur was a carpenter, and Percy was a clerk with the land valuation office. Although the family lived in Oxford, they did have a connection with London – George was born there. Was there a connection with Doris's family to Oxford? Yes, Fanny was born in Oxford.

Despite researching into the further branches of both family trees I was unable to find a blood connection. I did find a tree with a lovely photo of Harold in later years. He is the Harold in the tree I created but I can't prove he is Doris's Harold.

What exhibition had H Grant's father taken him to? The Japanese-British Exhibition was held in White City, London from May to October in 1910. Its opening was delayed by the death of Edward VII. By the time the event closed, more than 8 million people had visited – including H Grant and his father. Of course, I've assumed 'H' was a lad – but even that can't be confirmed.

Court of Honour, Coronation Exhibition, London, 1911

Dear Annie

Can you fancy us here at the Exhibition in London. We are staying with Glancy our address for the week is 11 the Strand Grove Park Rd Chiswick

Miss Marcus
c/o Dr Le Cronier
11 Midvale Rd
St Heliers
Jersey (CI)

051119

051119
June 1911
Miss Marcus
C/O Dr Le Cronier
11 Midvale Road
St Helier
Jersey
(CI)
Dear Annie
Can you fancy us here at the Exhibition in London.
We are staying with friends. Our address for the week is 11 The Strand, Grove Park Road, Chiswick.

There are one or two lessons within this story for any family historian who is uncertain or confused by what they discover – and dismiss or accept their findings.

I knew that the recipient of the postcard lived in Jersey and was there during the German occupation in the Second World War. However, I never found Anne with any of her close family in any preceding census returns.

In 1901, Anne Marcus (b.1876) was with her aunt and uncle – Elizabeth (b.1832) and James Aspinall (b.1833), a farmer – in Jersey. In 1891, she was a servant in Jersey for Ernest (b.1860) and Maud Briad (b.1866) and their family. Ernest was a general merchant. In 1881, she was with the Aspinalls in Liverpool. At that time James is listed as a coal dealer.

I tried several times to create Anne's tree and each time I became frustrated and deleted her parents and siblings – some of it just didn't seem to make sense. I focused on the aunt and uncle and created their tree with much more success. Elizabeth née Renouf was born in Jersey and from there I was able to fill in the gaps.

Anne was born in Dartmouth and I was able to find her family there, or so I hoped. Her father was John Marcus (b.1839) – a shoemaker. I also found him in a number of Royal Navy records. He and Anne's mother, Louisa, were born in Jersey – which sounded an acceptable detail. However, when I found their marriage records in 1867, John is listed as a professor of music – and a widower. His wife, Anne's mother, was Louisa Renouf (b.1841). I found John's first marriage in 1860 to Hannah née Miller (b.1835) – at this time he was a shoemaker.

I also discovered that his father was Benjamin Marcus (b.1799) – a clockmaker from either Russia or Prussia (there was conflicting evidence of this). Benjamin is found in various directories for Jersey as a clockmaker. His wife, John's mother, was Sophie née Countanch (b.1813) – born in Jersey.

So, had I the correct family for Anne? Could there be two families that had been mixed into one? I looked at some other online trees and found very limited results. None included John's first marriage – or the birth of a son within that marriage, George (b.1868).

Along with their father, George and a half-sibling, John (b.1873), also appear in naval records. George worked on ships as a tailor and his father was also there, making shoes.

John junior appears in a website: Dartmouth's Great War Fallen. This is a very detailed website with biographies of those killed in the war. I was surprised and relieved to see that much of my own research mirrored that for John and his family. The website suggests that although John senior was a professor of music, it simply meant that for a time he tried to earn a living through music. His trade was, as I had found, a shoemaker. However, he was also a member of HMS *Britannia*'s band. John junior was aboard HMS *Luciline* and lost his life when the ship was torpedoed by a U-boat in 1917. The site also mentioned that Benjamin was from Prussia.

I found very little about Anne – the recipient of the postcard. In 1911, she worked for retired surgeon John Le Cronier (b.1823) and his son, Hardwick Le Cronier (b.1857), who was also a surgeon. She never married and survived the German occupation of the Channel Islands.

Which exhibition had the sender of the postcard attended? The Festival of the Empire was held at Crystal Palace, London to celebrate the coronation of George V and opened on 12 May 1911.

Elite Gardens, Coronation Exhibition, London, 1911

CORONATION EXHIBITION, 1911.
OFFICIAL
POST CARD
Correspondence   Address

Dear To Edith
We are now at
White City very
hot day
            Clara

Mrs Thompson
13 Waterloo Rd
Norwich

052066

052066
5 June 1911
Mrs Thompson
13 Waterloo Road
Norwich
Dear xx & Edith
We are now at White City very hot day.
Clara.

Edith Thompson née Freestone (b.1875) and her husband William (b.1863) ran a grocery business in Norwich. Edith was the daughter of a bootmaker and grinder – William (b.1844) and Elizabeth (b.1846).

Edith had at least six siblings. Her brother William (b.1867) also worked with leather, and in 1911 he is listed as a leather merchant – and living with his wife, Isabella (b.1870). Emma (b.1870) married George Burrage (b.1872) – a general dealer. Gertrude (b.1883) married Frederick Cox (b.1878) – an ironmonger. Lily (b.1885) married Francis Jay (b.1884) – an insurance clerk. Clara, who I believe sent the card, married Joseph Piggin (b.1871) – a leather salesman.

I struggled to trace another sister, Alice (b.1865). However, in 1871, I found her living with her paternal grandmother – Alice (b.1821), a widow. The grandmother is listed as the licensee for the Red Lion in Magdalen Street, Norwich. The Norfolk Pubs website lists Alice as the licensee but with the name Hannah – the variance to the census is noted on the website. It also shows that previously William Freestone (b.1826) was the licensee. Knowing that Alice might have been Hannah Alice helped discover more about this earlier generation. I found the couple in 1861, in a different pub – The Wellington in Muspole Street. This was confirmed on the Norfolk Pubs website.

I'm not keen on going too far back without exploring the source documents. However, I was able to trace the family and discovered the couple had married on 25 December 1849. I also discovered Hannah Alice's maiden name: Warren. This fitted in very nicely with many of the children in the tree in the subsequent generations having this as a middle name – including Edith, the recipient of the postcard. Another document from their marriage told me that Hannah Alice was unable to sign her name. The final revelation which seemed to bring the story full-circle was her father's occupation – shoemaker.

The information on the Norfolk Pubs website was invaluable to this story. The website has a note: *The information is provided free as a reference to all – if used in other published works then reference to source would be appreciated.* I am very pleased to acknowledge their work.

Exposition de Bruxelles, 1910. Les Jardins Français

OFFICIELLE
ET INTERNATIONALE
BRUXELLES 1910

Miss Gill,
5 Devonshire Rd.
Gt Yarmouth.

053100

053100
1911
Miss Gill
5 Devonshire Road
Great Yarmouth
Dear A
Have been staying here since Sat: going tonight. I thought I must write to wish you every success in your new appointment. You will be sorry to hear that our little pet passed away a fortnight ago. Will write a letter later. Love to your mother and yourself.
Mabel J

In 1911, the widowed Elizabeth Gill née Barnes (b.1859) lived at the address with her unmarried sister, Mary (b.1860), and two sons – Alfred (b.1896) and Edgar (b.1899). At the age of 15, Alfred was a machine hand in a tinned fish factory.

Ten years earlier Elizabeth and her husband, Alfred (b.1860), lived at another address in Great Yarmouth. Alfred was a policeman and at the time of their marriage, his father, William Gill (b.1830), was a police sergeant.

Who was Miss A Gill? I searched and searched and couldn't find her. Elizabeth Gill declared in 1911 that she'd had five children. I had found five children: Elizabeth Diana (b.1888), George (b.1890), Frederick (b.1892), Alfred (b.1896) and Edgar (b.1899). In 1911, Elizabeth (also listed as Diana Elizabeth) was a boarder in Norfolk, employed as a teacher in a council school.

The family appeared to have a typical working class life. I even found Alfred in Massachusetts, America working as a chef – recorded in his American naturalization record of 1939. However, the family hadn't always enjoyed a relatively good life.

Elizabeth Gill's mother was Elizabeth née Hellenburgh (b.1840). Elizabeth Hellenburgh's father was Hans (b.1805), a sailor and fisherman. In 1871, he was a shrimp catcher. Hans and his wife, Mary née Rouse (b.1801), had at least four children. In 1881, he was an inmate of the town's workhouse and he died there in 1885. In 1903, one of his sons, Cornelius (b.1835), also died in the workhouse. It's sobering to realise that only a few years separated this family from poverty and destitution.

VIEW FROM KINNOULL HILL
PERTHSHIRE.

054071

054071
10 December 1911
Mrs Ephgrave
11 The Square, Wellington Street
Burton-on-Trent
River View
Invergowrie
Dear Mrs Ephgrave
Hearty birthday greetings and all best wishes for many happy returns! – I hope you are keeping well; I feel better since I came up here and enjoy my new position very much. With kindest regards.
H[?]

Eliza Ephgrave was born in December 1852. She's listed in various census returns as a widow with one son, George (b.1878). George was born in India and I struggled to trace any firm facts about him and his mother – apart from her birth in Hertfordshire.

In 1881, she was a schoolmistress in Denton, Sussex. Although she's listed as a widow, her title was Miss. George was with her at the address. He was with her 10 years later in Staffordshire where she was a small ware and general trader. In 1901, she was matron of the almshouse in Wellington Street – the address on the postcard in 1911.

In 1939 she was still a matron, this time at Belvedere House in Burton-upon-Trent.

The almshouses in Wellington Street were built in the 1870s. They were constructed in a distinctive Gothic style. The Consolidated Charity still runs 29 almshouses in the area – from listed buildings to modern bungalows. In 2016 the charity advertised for residents to fill spaces in their properties – including Wellington Street.

George appears in several passenger lists, sailing to and from America with his wife, Marion née Bennett. George had become an advertising manager and I found the family in Washington, DC. In a 1930 census return he is listed as president – although the original document has been struck-through. At that time he was still classified as an alien and English. The census declaration also confirmed that his father was English – although I had not found any definitive information about him. The date that George first arrived in America was given as 1899.

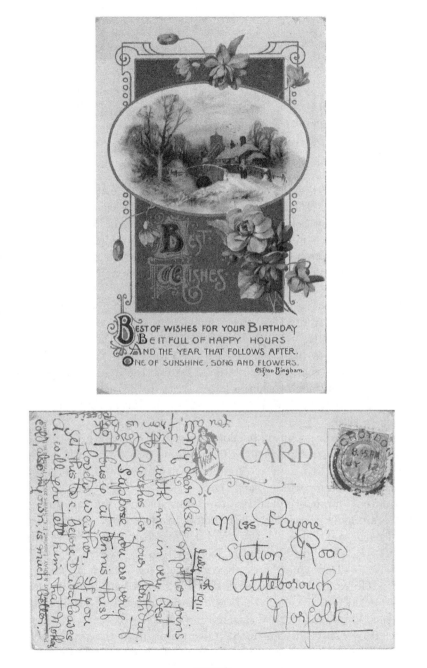

055055

055055
11 July 1911
Miss Payne
Station Road
Attleborough, Norfolk
My Dear Elsie
Mother joins with me in very best wishes for your birthday. Suppose you are very busy at tennis this lovely weather. If you get this PC before Dada leaves A will you tell him that Mother's cold, also my own, is much better.
With love to you all, from us both.
Bessie.

Elsie Payne (b.1891) lived with her parents William (b.1858) and Kate née Bedford (b.1858). William was a commercial traveller and sold drapery. Before that he had been a warehouseman and appears in the 1881 census return in London – in Fy Foot Lane. Listed at the address are almost one hundred fellow warehousemen. Fy Foot Lane doesn't appear on modern maps and seems to have been a narrow lane, not much more than a path, near the Thames.

William's father, also William (b.1828), was a bootmaker and his wife, Elizabeth née Watson (b.1833), was a milliner.

Elsie's mother, Kate née Bedford, wasn't a Norfolk girl. She was born in Shoreditch and was the daughter of a clerk to a news agent. Her brother, Thomas (b.1861), married Lavinia née Dean (b.1860) – the daughter of a gardener from Buckinghamshire – James Dean (b.1831). Thomas worked for the Poor Law Service as an Assistant Clerk to Guardians. Earlier he had been a solicitors' clerk.

The early 20th century heralded reform for welfare in the United Kingdom. The stigma attached to the workhouse was supposedly removed by a rebranding and renaming to Poor Law Institution in 1911 – at the time Thomas was working within that system.

Thomas's mother, Elizabeth (b.1834), answers the question about Thomas's middle name Pain – Elizabeth's maiden name. Yes, a family tree with Paynes and Pains. Thomas and Lavinia had one child – Elizabeth (b.1891) – Bessie. Is the Dada in the message Bessie's father?

I haven't always bought death certificates for anyone included in my research. However, as Bessie had died in 1914 – not long after she wrote the card – I decided to see what else I could find. The cause of death given was a TB-related illness and she had suffered from this for six years. Her death was registered by Daisy Basham (b.1889), a milliner from Essex. The cold that Bessie mentioned in her postcard was no trivial ailment. Elsie looked after the postcard – it's in almost perfect condition. This was such a sad story for a beautiful card.

056101

056101
1911
Shield Villa
Fitzwilliam Street
Peterborough
My dear Ethel
I am feeling quite well today hope you are quite well too. I am very busy today & will write
tomorrow.
Fondest love.
Yours ever
GBY
Victor

Very often when I'm looking for cards to research I will pass on the ones that are too difficult to read. Thank goodness I took a second look at this one. I doubt that even with the transcript you are able to read the message without difficulty. Using a mirror solves the problem – but what a task the writer had.

Ethel Wells was born in 1890 and in 1911 she lived at the address on the card with her parents, Robert (b.1838) and Martha née Foreman (b.1851). Martha was Robert's second wife. Sarah née Lilley (b.1837) died a year before Robert and Martha married in 1867 and is the mother to at least two children. Robert had a total of 12 children and he declared this in the 1911 census return – also that three had died.

Robert was employed in a number of jobs within the railway industry and by 1911 he was a retired railway engine driver. As a younger man he was a railway fireman.

Despite some of the children being born to his first wife, all are included in the total declared in 1911 – 12 born, nine surviving. As a check to ensure I had the correct family, I found the register for his marriage to Martha and it shows him as a widower and employed as an engine driver. This tallied with his occupation in the 1911 census: a retired railway engine driver.

In 1911, Ethel was a shop assistant working in millinery. In 1918 she married Walter Wingate (b.1890), who worked as a maintenance engineer in the generation of electricity.

MISS CHRISSIE WHITE
OF THE HEPWORTH STOCK COMPANY

057111

145

057111
13 January 1914
Miss Silvester
218 Upper Tooting Road
Tooting
London
Tuesday morning
Dear D
Many thanks for lovely present. I am delighted with it. You are good to do all that work for me. I shall look smart to-morrow. I expect you will be sorry to hear I scalded my foot on Saturday. It is very painful still. I upset kettle of boiling water over it and I am limping along like an old woman.
It has two

Daisy Silvester (b.1889) lived in Tooting with her sister, Maggie (b.1893), her mother, Sarah Finch née Bishop (b.1860), and her stepfather, Robert Finch (b.1867), who was a timber merchant. When the couple married in 1901, Sarah was a widow. Horatio Silvester (b.1860) had died in 1897. In 1891, the family lived in Peckham and Robert Finch was also at the address, as a lodger.

Horatio was a hairdresser and he had at least three brothers: James (b.1849), Frederick (b.1852) and Richard (b.1854).

James lived for a time on the Isle of Wight with his wife, Sarah (b.1863), and was a prison warder. He had at least three children and they were born on the island.

Frederick was also a hairdresser and although I found him eventually working in Dorset, he is listed in a London directory in 1895. In 1911, his widow, Louise (b.1858), lived in Dorset and their youngest son, Arthur (b.1892), is recorded as a hairdresser. By 1931, Arthur had become a tobacconist, confectioner, stationer and cycle agent in Cranborne.

Richard became a bricklayer, living in London with his family, including wife Ellen née Brewer (b.1849).

Horatio's parents were James (b.1826) and Maria née Chown (b.1816). James is listed as a manufacturer of harnesses and later of army accoutrements. In 1911, his occupation is given as army instrument maker. Much of his life was spent living in and around Chelsea. At the time of his marriage to Maria in 1848, he had been unable to sign his name and his occupation was given as a saddler.

What became of Daisy and her sister Maggie? There were several possible sightings after 1911, but they all led back to a different branch of the tree. I did discover another sister via a baptism record. Ethel Silvester was born in 1883 and died four years later.

Who sent the card? That also led nowhere and I can't help wondering what the incomplete final sentence was leading to – *It has two...?*

View of Cheddar.

058045

058045
31 Gloucester Square
Hyde Park
London
26 February 1915
Mrs Steers
37 Layton Road
Brentford
Middlesex
Dear Sister & Brother
Just a PC to say I will be over on Sunday to tea – hope you are all well.
Love to you all.
Hilda
XXX

Mrs Steers was Rose Ettie née Salisbury and she was born in 1877. In her baptism records, her mother, Rose Anna Salisbury (b.1857), is listed as a single woman and no details of the child's father are provided.

As I searched the various records, I discovered there were two Rose Anna Salisburys born in the same year in Brentford. One remained unmarried and worked as a charwoman. The other married and had several children with her husband Thomas Batty (b.1857). Which was my Rose?

The answer was found in Rose Steers' own marriage. She married Henry Steers (b.1878) in 1901, and the register shows a witness – Francis William Salisbury. I surmised he was either Rose's brother or uncle.

Back to Rose Batty. She married Thomas Batty in 1880 and they had at least four children: Emma (b.1881), Francis (b.1883), Thomas (b.1886) and Edward (b.1888). I reviewed each child's baptism records and Edward was baptised in 1888 on the same day as Winifred Amy Salisbury (b.1888) – whose father was Francis William Salisbury, a bricklayer. Both families lived in Coningsby Road. I felt that coincidence suggested I had the correct Rose. Of course, it could be just that – a coincidence. Other trees didn't help me – they had Rose, the mother, being born in Wiltshire and elsewhere.

Now I was fairly confident I had the correct family members I was able to discover a little more about them. Rose, the recipient of the postcard, had eight children. Her husband, Henry Steers, was a gas fitter. Henry's parents were John (b.1853) and Eliza Steers (b.1854) and they had at least seven children, including Henry. Their youngest was Hilda (b.1892) – who sent the postcard. In 1911, Hilda lived with another brother, Joseph (b.1886), and his wife, Mary (b.1877). Joseph was a motor omnibus driver and Hilda is listed as a horse keeper. However, I believe that to be a combination of bad handwriting and bad transcribing and that she was actually a housekeeper.

In 1920, Hilda married Alfred King (b.1889), an electrician. The couple emigrated to America and appear in passenger lists for that same year. Hilda died in Pennsylvania in the 1970s.

Although I knew she wasn't at the address in 1911, I wondered who might have lived at the Gloucester Square property. Bernice Abenheim (b.1877) was an American and wife of Richard Abenheim (b.1867), also an American. In 1901, he is listed as an import/export merchant. Although I found the family in various passenger lists, they were still in London in 1939. At this time Richard was a metal and steel importer/exporter. Bernice was originally from San Francisco and she died in London in 1949.

I reviewed other family trees and some suggested that Bernice was the daughter of Adolph Hirschman (b.1839) from Germany and Regina née Geigermann (b.1853) from Prussia. Both parents were easily traced. However, I was now following a very tenuous link to the original postcard and had no evidence that Hilda had even worked for the family – as lovely as that would have been to confirm. That's perhaps a lesson to all genealogists – know when to stop!

I was surprised by the ultimate result of the original family. We all have impressions of unmarried mothers in the 19th century and how they were treated, but how unusual was it for an unmarried mother to eventually marry and have a family?

Bournemouth from Pier

Miss L. Burkinshaw
32. Greenfoot Lane
Old-Town. Barnsley
Yorkshire

059029

059029
8 July 1910
Miss L Burkinshaw
32 Greenford Lane
Old Town
Barnsley, Yorkshire
My dear Laura
Hope this finds you well. Received yours this morning today. Yes the paper will always be
welcome. I'll write letter soon. Best regards and wishes to all.
Best L to you.
CLS Edwin
HMS [?]
GPO London

Laura Burkinshaw was born in 1884 and her parents were Samuel (b.1836) and Sarah née Briggs (b.1849). In 1911, Laura lived with her widowed mother who was a certified midwife – 10 years earlier she was a charwoman. Samuel was a labourer.

Edwin (b.1883) was born in Barnsley and began his naval career in 1899. Before that he was a collier – which he would later return to. In 1939 he is listed as an incapacitated underground coalminer.

Laura and Edwin married in 1912 and as interesting as their lives had been to research, it was Edwin's ancestors that had a more fascinating story to share. His parents were James (b.1865) and Rhoda née Jervis (b.1864).

Edwin's family name was Heppenstall Crapper and I wondered if there was any connection between the family and Thomas Crapper, of flushing toilet fame. Although I failed to find a connection, it did allow me to explore Edwin's family. I was surprised to discover that Edwin's grandfather was James Heppenstall (b.1818) – no mention of Crapper.

The 1871 census reveals that James was a widower and living in Barnsley with Lydia Crapper (b.1825). Her marital status was also widow and her relation to the head of the household was mistress. Living in the home were Ann Heppenstall (b.1859), James Heppenstall Crapper (b.1865) – Edwin's father – and Hannah Heppenstall Crapper (b.1869).

In 1861, Lydia was married to Thomas Crapper (b.1806), a coalminer, and living with their children Tedber (b.1847), Mary (b.1850), Celina (b.1858) and Thomas (b.1861).

In 1851, Lydia is married to Thomas, and living with them are their children, including Tedber Taylor – listed as Thomas's stepson. Taylor was Lydia's maiden name. I found Tedber's baptism records and his details are: Tedber Bennett Taylor. There is no named father.

Did Lydia and James Heppenstall ever marry? There's no trace of such an event and an entry in a coroner's notebook, dated August 1883, confirms the status of the relationship (reproduced by kind permission of West Yorkshire Archive Service).

Lydia Crapper deceased

James Heppenstall of Pogmoor, Barnsley greengrocer says:

I have been living with deceased for the last 20 years she was 57 years old and the widow of Thomas Crapper a farm labourer.

She has been subject to attacks of spasms during the last 5 years and also to palpitations of the heart.

She has not had a doctor to visit her for some years past but she went several times to the hospital and dispensary a few months ago for spasms.

She was [?] last Tuesday at Barnsley last Wednesday and was washing at home last Thursday.

She ate her meals as usual and went to bed about 8 o'clock last Thursday night and seemed to sleep and rest nicely.

About a quarter past 3 o'clock yesterday morning I was awoke by hearing a rattling in her throat. I spoke to her and shook her and raised her up and shouted to my son James [Edwin's father] *who is 19 years old and he fetched in some neighbour women but deceased died directly.*

Her life is insured in the office of the Prudential Assurance Company.

Signed JH.

Again, this is another story that sheds a different light on illegitimacy. Lydia had given birth to Tedber as a single woman. She had then married Thomas Crapper and had a family with her husband – and her illegitimate son was part of that family. After her husband's death, she began a relationship with James Heppenstall and had more children.

It doesn't seem that any of that was a secret – listing her as a mistress in a census return seems a bold admission. Also, James confirms in his statement that she was the widow of Thomas Crapper – and not his own wife. Their children were given Lydia's married name of Crapper – so perhaps everyone knew of their mother's status.

A choice Line of Useful and Adornamental Articles.

POST CARD.

COMMUNICATION.

ADDRESS.

Dear Ernie. You are
a long time sending me a
P. Card. This is real thy
day people here hang them
in the bed.
I'm just going to Reading
with my friend, I am to meet
Rin you here a Cathedrale.
Last Saturday with love
to all from Bela.

Mr Walker
Eastcliffe House
Morton Road
S. Lowestoft

060130

153

060130
17 May 1911
Mr Walker
Eastcliffe House
Morton Road
Lowestoft
Dear Ernie
You are a long time sending me a postcard. This is how they dry clothes here, hang them in the street. I'm just going to Dewsbury with my friend, going to market. Did you have a hot short cake last Saturday. With love to all from Gert.

In 1911, Ernest Walker (b.1885) was a shop assistant, working for his uncle and aunt – George Forster (b.1859) and Jane née Walker (b.1858). George and Jane's only child – Gertrude (b.1884), a shop assistant – was also living at the address.

Ernest's father, William Walker (b.1859), had at least nine children with his first wife, Annie née Boon (b.1860). In the 1920s the couple and their children appear in a census return in Canada. After Annie's death he married again – Lydia née Parker (b.1859) – in Utah, where he would eventually become a naturalised citizen. After Lydia's death, William married Hannah née Johnson (b.1861).

Ernest, who received the postcard, became a milkman.

Who sent the postcard? It would be easy to assume that it must be Gertie, his cousin. However, Ernest had a sister, also named Gertrude (b.1894). Could it have been from her? In 1911, she was also living in Lowestoft working as a domestic day girl. Unfortunately I found nothing that could confirm which Gert it was.

4.U H.M. KING GEORGE V. ROTARY PHOTO. E.C

POST CARD

The Address only to be
Written Here.

Got caught in the rain
last night going home.
See you to-night as soon as
possible after 7. & two
returned.
W. B.L. A K. T.
George. xxx
           xxx

Miss E. Tommins,
32, Percy Street,
Hull

061043

061043
1911
Miss E Tommins
32 Percy Street
Hull
Got caught in the rain last night going home.
See you to night as soon as possible after 7. C has returned.
WBLAKF [With Best Love And Kisses Forever]
George
XXXXXX

You can't see it in the image here, but George is a romantic soul – he has used passionate red ink for the message – and what lovely writing the man has.

I found Evelyn Tommins (b.1892) in the 1911 census as a mother's help living with her family. I don't believe I've ever found a family with so many interesting occupations. Her father, Thomas Tommins (b.1863), was a baker and confectioner. Evelyn's uncle also lived with the family and Arthur Dixon (b.1851) was a watchmaker. Her brothers, Albert (b.1887) and Arthur (b.1889), were a shoemaker and joiner, respectively. Her sister, Hilda (b.1896), was a surgical dresser. I believe, based on the location, that Hilda worked in a factory where dressings were made. Two younger sisters, Doris (b.1899) and Lillian (b.1905), were at school.

Evelyn was born in Hull. Her mother, Clara née Dixon (b. 1867), was the daughter of a bank clerk, James Dixon (b.1830). Siblings of Clara worked as engineers in the bakery industry and in printing. As I mentioned earlier, this tree covers so many fascinating areas of employment.

Doris, Evelyn's sister, married Kenneth Brook (b.1900). Kenneth and his brother, Bernard (b.1899), were musicians. Their father, Frederick (b.1867), was a professor of music.

In 1911, George Baggley (b.1890) was a boarder living with William (b.1853) and Mary Shaw (b.1855). George was employed as a tinner for a drum maker. William, his landlord, was a stoker with Hull Oxide Co.

George was the son of a labourer – Samuel Baggley (b.1853). His mother was Jane née Elsworth (b.1852).

Evelyn and George married in 1915 – four years after he sent the postcard. There's more romance to add to this story. The placement of stamps on letters has a code and George's secret message, tilting the stamp as you see it, is: *I am faithful to you.* I found other explanations, but all involved similarly worded terms of endearment (see page 18).

In 1939 Evelyn's mother, Clara, lived with the couple. George had had a change of career by this time and was working as a secretary accountant to an engineering company.

Hampden Park, Eastbourne.

POST CARD.

THIS SPACE FOR INLAND
COLONIAL, AND CERTAIN
FOREIGN CORRESPONDENCE

THE ADDRESS ONLY TO
BE WRITTEN HERE

22 avondale Rd

Dear Teacher
I am sending you a
card, thank you very
much for my pretty
card I hope you will
soon be back with us
I am sorry I have not
sent before
    Love from your
    Little Scholar
    Bessie Botting

Miss Lane
Devonshire House
Prince Town
S Devon

062049

062049

30 August 1910
Miss Lane
Devonshire House
Prince Town
S Devon
Dear Teacher
I am sending you a card thank you very much for my pretty card. I hope you will soon be
back with us. I am sorry I have not sent before.
Love from your little scholar.
22 Avondale Road
Eastbourne

In 1911, Bessie Botting lived with her parents, John (b.1874) and Lizzie née Ford (b.1874), at Avondale Road. John was a drainer working for a builder. His father, Henry (b.1846), was an agricultural carter. In 1891, Lizzie worked as a servant for a retired major in the Royal Sussex Regiment.

The couple had five children: Bessie (b.1900), Beatrice (b.1903), Albert (b.1904), William (b.1906) and Margaret (b.1910).

In 1923 Bessie married Ernest Greenfield, a butcher. Beatrice married a corporation dustman.

Who was Miss Lane?

Searching the address didn't find her. I then looked at the 1901 census, searching for an unmarried teacher in Eastbourne with the surname Lane. It didn't take too long to find someone who could be Bessie's Miss Lane. Helen Lane was born in Cornwall in 1869. In 1901, she was a governess to a family in Selwyn Road. However, after an hour or so I realised that the transcriber had made a mistake and instead of finding Miss Lane, I had found a Miss *Jane*. Miss Jane was the daughter of a vicar and they lived in Devon. It was very satisfying creating her tree – although it didn't help me with my search! I looked for any Miss Lanes in Eastbourne or Devon – and found several.

Miss Lane had kept Bessie's postcard, so whoever she was, she appreciated Bessie's efforts. I think it's rather touching that Miss Lane had also sent a card to Bessie. I wonder what happened to that one?

063056

063056

17 December 1915

Mr C Wallington

82 Manchester Rd

Swindon

Wilts

Dear Cyril

Many thanks for your letter. I liked the "French".

Well, I really cannot think of anything I want and don't you spend your money on me. Fancy you having 3 weeks holiday, we have until Wednesday morning. Please give my love to Auntie and thank her very much for letter. Sorry I did not write to you yesterday but I was very busy helping Mother. G'pa is about the same. Hope you will have Reg home for Christmas. I cannot realise it is next week. We are very busy, expect all shops are just now. much love.

Doris.

Cyril Wallington was born in 1901 in Wiltshire and his brother, Reginald (b.1896), was serving in the First World War at the time the postcard was sent.

On 6 November 1915 Reginald is listed with the Royal Naval Air Service and served on HMS *President II*. He also appears in records for the RAF (presumably because the RNAS would eventually be merged with the Royal Flying Corps to form the Royal Air Force in 1918).

Reginald had a degree in engineering and in 1911 he joined Great Western Railway as a draughtsman. Cyril would also work for the railway and is recorded as a maintenance fitter in a railway workshop.

Cyril and Reginald's father was George Wallington (b.1871) and he was a railway clerk. His father, Cyril and Reginald's grandfather, was Francis Wallington (b.1835), a railway engine driver.

In 1939 the brothers lived with their mother, Maud née Hall (b.1874). Her father, James Hall (b.1830), was a builder.

Despite creating trees for Cyril's parents, I was unable to trace Doris. The parents had 11 siblings between them and although I looked at the marriages for the siblings I couldn't trace a Doris. Of course, it's highly possible that she fell between the census returns. However, she didn't appear in any trees that I was able to access. Was she even a relative? I had thought she might have been a cousin but even a quick sweep of all births within the obvious parameters didn't find her. Perhaps Doris was her middle name.

Tilly Whim Caves, Swanage

August 28th
Ferndene
Cranborne Rd
Swanage Dorset
Dear Mr H, thanks for
yours am sorry you had
a lovely walk on Sunday,
Today it is a grand day,
so rough, we went up
to the caves it was
awful the wind took
us off our feet twice
We felt it for that although
walk each day although
full of comfort by kind
regards to Mr H & Mrs
are so pleased for

Mr M Hookes
83 Bernard Street
St Albans
Herts

064004

161

064004

28 August 1910

33 Bernard Street

St Albans

Dear M thanks for yours, am sorry you had a lonely walk on Sunday. Today it is a [?] so rough, we up to these caves. It was awful, the wind took us off our feet twice. We start out for that walk each day although [?] of [?].

Ferndene, Cranborne Road, Swanage, Dorset.

I wasn't certain I could identify the recipient of this card – the family had nine children. However, I completed a brief tree for them and followed the lives of some of the family members.

In 1881, Frederick Hooker (b.1849) and Frances née Sears (b.1847) lived in Bernard Street with their children, William (b.1873), Lilian (b.1875), Frank (b.1877), Arthur (b.1879) and Minnie (b.1880). Frederick was a groom and Frances was a hat trimmer. Also living with them were Fanny (b.1799) and Susan Sears (b.1843) – Frances's mother and sister, respectively. Fanny was also a hat trimmer.

In 1901, the children still in Bernard Street were Lily, Frank, Alfred (b.1882), Ralph (b.1884) and Maud (b.1886). Lily was now a straw hat finisher and Alfred was a straw hat packer. Frank was a painter.

In 1911, a year after the card was sent, Lily, Frank, Ralph and Maud were still living at home. The girls worked in the straw hat industry and the boys were painters.

In 1939, 58 years after the family's first appearance in the census returns at Bernard Street, the family still lived in the same house. Now it was William's turn to be head of the household, living with his wife, Annie (b.1871). William was a jobbing gardener.

Lilian never married and in 1939 she was still working as a hat finisher and living with her sister, Maud, and her husband, Walter White (b.1882) – a hospital porter.

In 1911, Ferndene was occupied by Annie Bushill (b.1863). Also living at the address was her sister, Ellen Bushill (b.1865). In 1901, they lived at Ferndene with their mother, Elizabeth (b.1838).

The sisters were born in Coventry and before moving to Swanage, lived with their mother and brother, Frederick (b.1867), in Westbourne – now part of Bournemouth, Dorset. Elizabeth was born in London but appears in earlier census returns in the Coventry area with her children.

I have to admit an interest in this particular postcard. I lived in Swanage for 30 years and I know the area very well. Ferndene was a detached property in a quiet road where several houses offered accommodation – later becoming guest houses. The house has been demolished and redeveloped into flats – as has the Westbourne property in Alum Chine Road.

Next door to Ferndene lived the Tunnell family and during my very early life, I attended Betty Tunnell's dance classes – even participating (dancing would be too much of a reach) in the shows the classes performed in a local theatre.

Betty (b.1899) was a former actress and had clearly retained her contacts. One memorable show was *Ali Baba* and the local press noted that some of the costumes had come from the 1960s epic film *Cleopatra* starring Elizabeth Taylor (b.1932). My mother made my costumes – and what an excellent job she did!

So as to prevent the straw from drying and becoming stiff, the workers would moisten it with saliva, causing sores to fingers and lips – Tracing Your Trade & Craftsman Ancestors, Adèle Emm

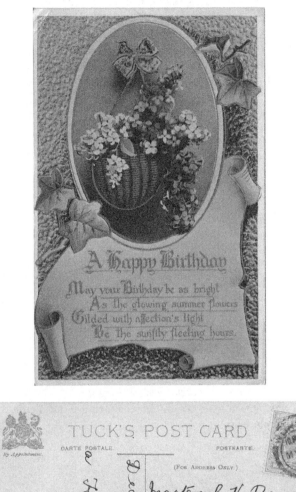

065033

Birthday Greetings

May all your ways
be pleasant ways,
And all your days
be happy days.

TUCK'S POST CARD

CARTE POSTALE.

POSTKARTE

(FOR ADDRESS ONLY)

Dear Cecil,
With all good
wishes for a
happy Birthday
love from
Connie

Master C. V. Berry
14 Bridge Place.
Worksop.

065033

165

065033

6 May 1910

Master CV Berry

14 Bridge Place, Worksop

Dear Cecil

Wishing you a Happy Birthday.

Love from

F Blundell

May 1910

Dear Cecil

With all good wishes for a happy Birthday.

Love from Connie

In 1911, Cecil (b.1894) lived with his parents, Joseph (b.1859) and Edith née Torr (b.1864), and his brother, Joseph (b.1892). Joseph senior was a pianoforte tuner and dealer. Cecil's brother Joseph was an apprentice chemist and Cecil was a student of music. The family were living at the same address 10 years earlier, and with them was Cecil's grandmother, Emma Berry née Fullard (b.1841).

The family had strong connections with Bridge Place. Cecil's paternal grandfather was also named Joseph (b.1831), and in 1891 he's recorded as a gunsmith – living at 24 Bridge Place with Emma. The family were also at that address 20 years earlier.

All of the census returns show that Emma was born in Whitwell, Derbyshire. However, when I reviewed the suggested hints, she appears in several trees as being born in Staffordshire – with a different year of birth. In the trees where she is listed as being born in Whitwell, the year of birth is 1841 – as I have. Those other trees mirror mine in everything except that detail, sending the family off into another county with a different Emma – both with the maiden name Fullard.

Edith Torr's father was John Torr (b.1837) – listed in 1881 as an accountant. Her mother was Jane (b.1841) and the couple had at least five children, including Edith. Edith's youngest sister was Emily (b.1876). She married Geoffrey Blundell (b.1875) who was a brewery's clerk. They had at least two children, including Francis (b.1899) and Constance (b.1902) – the senders, perhaps, of the two postcards.

What became of Cecil and Joseph? They both served in the Royal Army Medical Corps during the First World War. Joseph completed his apprenticeship and became a pharmacist. Cecil continued with music and became a retail music dealer. Joseph married Laure née Aubert (b.1899) in 1925. A week later, Cecil married Laure's sister, Lucienne (b.1902). The sisters were from Belgium.

Cecil appears in several trade directories, including one from 1941 which confirms he was a 'music & musical instrument seller' – at 23 Bridge Place. Before that, in 1914, he was a music seller at number 14. Although Cecil's business continued into more recent times, when I looked online the shop in Bridge Place is now a Subway.

Deltiology, the formal name for postcard collecting – Various

Shaldon Beach

81 Ringmore Road
Shaldon
    S. Devon.

POST CARD

FRITH'S SERIES

My dear Katie I wish
you a very happy birthday
this is the sweetest place,
& the quaintest village,
& the scenery lovely, but
oh! for a breath of the Down
we can't stand it, G. looks
so ill & I have perpetual
neuralgia, so we go next
week, to 11 North Street
Sandown. I of Wight. We
climb round this point to
bathe & hide behind rocks
for machines. Can't get the
tent round. Best love M. H.

This Space may be used for Communication

The Address only to be written here

Miss H. B. Weston
Little Thurlow
Hayward's Heath
    Sussex.

TEIGNMOUTH
9 PM
JU 18
10

066006

168

066006
June 1910
81 Ringmore Road, Shaldon
Miss KB Weston
Little Thurlow
Haywards Heath
Sussex

My dear Katie, I wish you a very happy birthday. This is the sweetest place and the quaintest village and the scenery lovely, but oh! for a breath of the downs.
We can't stand. G. looks so ill and I have perpetual neuralgia, so we go next week to 11 North Street, Sandown, I of Wight. We climb round this point to bathe and hide behind rocks for machines. Can't get the tent round.
Best love MH

In 1911, Kate Bilhah Weston (b.1855) lived at the address on the card with her sister, Lillah Beata Weston (b.1846). The sisters were daughters of Henry Weston (b.1797) and his second wife Emily née Burgess (b.1812). In earlier census returns, Henry is listed as a banker. In 1881, he is recorded as a magistrate.

The couple had at least eight children. Percy Blandford Weston (b.1847) was a mining engineer and he married Katharine née Allen (b.1869) in 1911. The other children were: Lilla (b.1846), Frank (b.1850), Henrietta (b.1852), Kate (b.1854) – who received the card, and Herbert (b.1858). The eldest child was Dyson Weston (b.1844). Their half-sibling was Emma (b.1823).

In 1871, Dyson was living as a lodger in Liverpool, employed as first officer on a steamship.

In the 1936 *Shipping Wonders of the World* (a 55-part magazine series published by The Amalgamated Press Ltd), he gets more than a passing mention in an article detailing the engineering developments that led to the bilge keel – 'Motion of the Ship at Sea':

Another name closely associated with the development of the bilge keel is that of Mr Dyson Weston who in the 1870s was made the Marine Superintendent of the African Steamship Company. That concern owned a steamer called the Almera which had been built to cross the bars of West African ports.
Her draught was shallow and the bar keel, which was still customary, was replaced by a plate. She rolled so terribly that she was regarded as being positively dangerous and nobody would travel in her if it could possibly be avoided. The directors decided to sell her but the loss was considerable and it started Weston thinking. Froude's [William Froude (b.1810) naval architect] experiments were then in their early stages and had been principally confined to men-of-war. Weston adapted the principles to merchant ships and vastly improved the comfort of the traders to the west coast of Africa.

Dyson's association with the African Steamship Company hadn't come up in any of my searches. The company was founded in 1852 by Macgregor Laird (b.1808), brother of John Laird (b.1805) of shipbuilding fame, and based in Birkenhead – where Catherine was born in 1881.

How did I come across the article? My father saved the complete set of the magazine series – all 55 – from a skip. My parents kept them for more than 50 years, taking them from house to house each time they moved. I had no idea that the postcard that began this story had any connection to ships and sailing – and it was only as I completed this story that I decided to check the magazine index. Research success can be luck – and the ability to store ephemera for no apparent reason.

Back to Dyson and still in the 1870s, he appears in the crew list for *Mandingo*. He married Jane née Brown (b.1855) in 1876. By 1881, he is listed in a trade directory as a steamship owner. Other reports show him as a director of Stumore, Weston and Co. – a company that owned steamships, including SS *Dallam Tower* (launched 1880), SS *Barden Tower* (launched 1881), SS *Maulkins Tower* (launched 1882) and SS *Lilburn Tower* (launched 1883).

The company gets a mention in *History of the Zulu War* by Arthur Wilmot – published in 1879. Unfortunately a reprint of the book, published in 2013 by Cordar Books Ltd, doesn't carry that section. However, the company was mentioned in the original version in the context of carrying freight and passengers.

By 1911, Dyson had retired and lived with his wife and two of his children in Shipbourne, Kent. Dyson and Jane had four children in total. Henry Burgess Weston (b.1877) is listed in 1911 as being a composer of music. Jane (b.1879) was an artist. Their other children were Catherine (b.1881) and Lena (b.1882).

I found Henry, Jane and Lena living in Rock Farm House, Kent in 1939. Also with them was their aunt – Katie – the recipient of the postcard. Henry was a retired managing director and had worked for the fisheries organization.

I discovered more about this branch of the family in the online St Giles and Shipbourne Newsletter – produced to share local information and history. I found the family mentioned in a 2016 article.

Dyson and Jane Weston had moved to The Grange – a mansion that has not survived into this century. During the First World War the couple helped raise funds for good causes including 'comforts for wounded soldiers... in 1916 the eldest daughter, Miss [Jane] Weston, was secretary to The West Kent Women's Agricultural Committee working to encourage food production for the country'. The article also mentions the other children by name: Henry, Jane, Lena and Hilda (Hilda was Catherine's second name).

The next part created a problem for me and my own research: 'Harry, at the age of 38, enlisted as a Lieutenant in the 2nd Co Essex and Suffolk Royal Garrison Artillery. His name was in the "Shipbourne Absent Voters List of

1918" indicating that he was still in service although he subsequently returned safely to Shipbourne after the war. Sadly Harry Weston was killed following a motorcycle accident in Hildenborough in 1920'.

Was Harry Henry? And if he had been killed in 1920, who was living with the two sisters and Katie, the aunt, in 1939?

When Dyson Weston died in 1931, his probate records mention 'Henry Burgess Weston, farmer'. Jane Weston died in 1933 and her probate records also mention Henry being a farmer and the address given is Rock Farm, Kent. In 1941, when Katie died, he is also mentioned in her probate records – as being a retired fruit farmer.

I could only find a death for Henry Burgess Weston in 1967 – and the probate records give Rock Farm as his address. I searched in 1920 for 'Weston' and could not find any that matched the death mentioned in the newsletter – I even expanded the search to several years before and after 1920. Several trade directories list Westons (Kent) Ltd as fruit growers at various locations, including Rock Farm.

So, although the newsletter's article contributed to my Weston story, it does indicate how easy mistakes creep into local and family history. Rock Farm is less than 10 miles from Shipbourne and I'm sure there must have been a good reason for Harry/Henry's early demise to have been recorded in the local history. Perhaps it was based on an anecdote – something all family historians should beware of. What is the truth? I present here only the facts that I have discovered – I hope my story has the correct ending for Henry and he actually lived a long and fruitful life.

The 1916 Representation of the People Act ruled that members of the armed forces should be listed in separate registers under the constituencies in which they normally lived. The Absent Voter Lists enabled servicemen and women to vote by proxy or by postal application, when away from home on active service – Ancestry.co.uk

067091

067091
1914
Miss E Leak
12 Westwood St
Off Lady Pit Lane
Leeds
Yorks
Dear Friend
I am enjoying myself up to the mark. Hope you are doing the same.
I remain your sincere friend
William.
Don't be offended.

Edith (b.1895) lived with her parents, Thomas Leak (b.1866) and Mary née Skellington (b.1868). Her father was a coalminer and Edith was a mule piecer in a cloth mill (the work would have involved repairing broken threads, clearing the machines of debris and generally supporting the weavers).

Also living at the address were Thomas and Mary's six other children (two children had died by 1911): George, a waiter (b.1891), Annie, a button sewer (b.1896), William (b.1898), Nellie (b.1901) and Clara (b.1906).

Thomas was the son and grandson of miners. His father, George Leak (b.1837), married Ann née Bywater (b.1840) in 1861, and the couple lived with her parents, Joseph (b.1804) and Ann Bywater née Berry (b.1801), in 1861. Another researcher's tree led me to the fact that Joseph worked in a mill from the age of nine. My own searches found a Joseph R Bywater in Holbeck workhouse in 1871, recorded as a bleacher and an incapacitated imbecile. Was this Ann's father? I believe so. In 1861, his occupation is recorded as a linen bleacher. In 1871, Ann senior was living with her daughter, Ann Leak.

But what of Edith and her siblings?

I found many links suggesting Edith's married name was Speight. However, when I looked at the actual marriage records, they showed this Edith's father as being a painter and deceased at the time of the marriage. I couldn't ignore the mining references in the census returns. Closer investigation proved worthwhile. Those trees also gave different siblings and a different mother – confirming one can't just add a branch because the name and dates of your main subject fit.

I decided to focus on the siblings – hoping something might lead me to Edith and even find her with a William.

In 1920 William married Gerty née Horsfield (b.1894), the daughter of a coal dealer. At this time William was a miner and it shows in their marriage records they both lived at the address on the postcard. In 1939 William was still a miner.

In 1928, Nellie sailed for Canada on the *Montnairn*. A month later, in Ontario, she married Horace Clough (b.1899), a painter from England. In 1911, Horace was living with his family in Nottinghamshire. His father, William (b.1874), was a boot riveter and later a shop inspector. His eldest brother, Norman (b.1898), was killed in the First World War and is buried in France. Horace's eldest sister, Gladys (b.1905), married Ernest Hinchcliffe, a bank clerk. In 1958, Gladys sailed on *Queen Mary* to New York.

In 1938 Nellie sailed to Glasgow as a passenger on the *Athenia* with her daughter. Their address is given as Beeston – where the family were from.

In 1948, Horace, Nellie and their daughter sailed back to England 'tourist class' aboard *Elizabeth*. Horace is recorded as a building inspector and their daughter is an office girl. A month later they returned to Canada on *Queen Mary*. The daughter is listed as a cashier.

Despite tracing members of the family in this country and abroad, I never did trace an Edith I was happy to include – or her sincere friend William.

The Archangel Gabriel, bringer of messages, is patron saint of postal workers and the Post Office – The Postal Museum

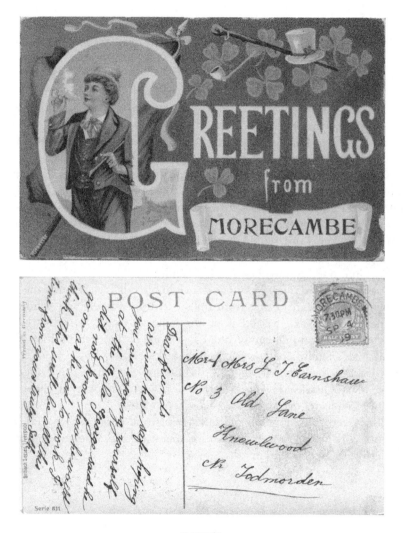

068052

175

068052
4 September 1909
Mr and Mrs LT Earnshaw
No 3 Old Lane
Knowlwood
Nr Todmorden
Dear friends
Arrived here safe hoping you are enjoying yourself at the gala. George said he did not know how he would go or as he had to work I think this will be all this time from yours truly Seth.

Lord Thomas Earnshaw (b.1877) lived at the address on the card with his wife, Susannah née Quayle (b.1876). However, with the occupation of carter it was soon clear that No 3 Old Lane was not a stately pile.

Was Lord a nickname? I began by creating his tree and found that his father was Thomas Earnshaw (b.1853), a coalminer. Lord's mother was Mary née Clegg (b.1855). Going further back, I discovered Lord's paternal grandfather was also Lord Earnshaw (b.1824) – and a blacksmith. In 1813 his father, John Earnshaw (b.1789), had married Mary née Lord (b.1791) – the answer to the naming puzzle.

In 1845, when Lord senior married Margaret née Holt (b.1827), neither could sign their names – nor could their witnesses. Lord senior had followed his father into trade and worked as a blacksmith.

Looking at Lord and Susannah's neighbours it's clear that the main employment in the area came from mills – cotton weavers and winders are prominent. In fact, as I walked along the Lane via the 1911 census I found little evidence of non-mill employment – just one bootmaker. Further away, a fish salesman's family all worked in mill-related jobs.

Lord and Susannah married in 1906. During Susannah's childhood, her mother, Mary Quayle née Halstead (b.1847), was a shopkeeper and grocer. Her father, William Quayle (b.1842), had died in 1880.

I discovered a photograph of Earl's headstone online. It's a very fancy piece of work and I'm sure there are many people who've seen it and considered him to be a lord in title.

069061

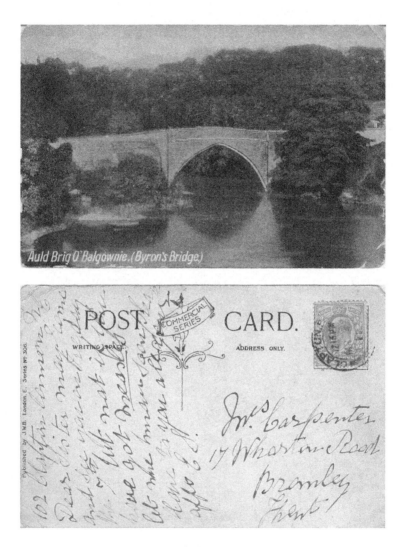

Auld Brig O'Balgownie. (Byron's Bridge.)

069061

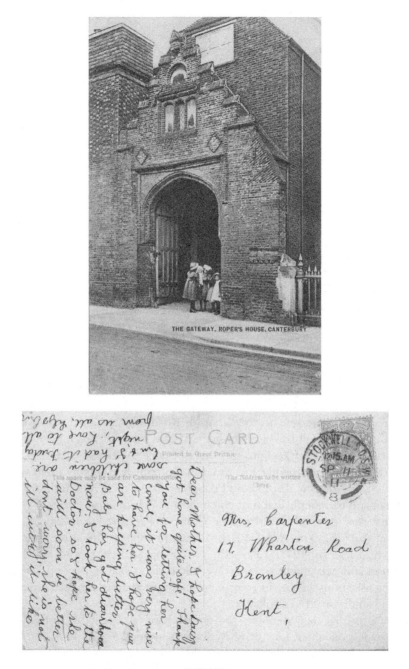

THE GATEWAY, ROPER'S HOUSE, CANTERBURY

069061

069061
13 June 1911
Miss Carpenter
17 Wharton Road
Bromley
Kent
St Rose Ward
Dear Daisy
Just a line to say I am all right this morning. I could not sleep much. There are 26 beds in our room and over 100 women in the home. We are not allowed to speak at meal times. I had milk pudding for supper.
Send love [?]

September 1911
Mrs Carpenter
Dear Mother.
I hope Daisy got home quite safe. Thank you for letting her come, it was very nice to have her. I hope you are keeping better. Baby has got diarrhoea now. I took her to the doctor so I hope she will soon be better. Don't worry, she is not ill with it like some children are. Ern and I had it Friday night. Love to all from us all. Lily and Ernest.

September 1911
Mrs Carpenter
Dear Sister, may come and see you on Friday the 7th but not if you have measles. Let me know soon please. Love to you all your affectionate E.S.

All three cards were sent to the Wharton Road address and I opted to buy them because they all followed the same theme – health. Also, as much as I know I can't keep all collections together, it is nice to keep at least these three.

In 1911, Mary Carpenter née Stretton (b.1858) lived at the address with her husband Anthony (b.1858) and daughter Daisy (b.1890). Anthony was a postman and the couple had four children. By 1911, one had died.

Mary was one of five daughters born to Thomas (b.1823) and Ann Stretton (b.1825). The eldest was Elizabeth (b.1853) – the sister concerned about measles. In 1911, Elizabeth was living with a family in Clapton Common and working as a cook. Over the earlier decades I found Elizabeth working as a housekeeper in Kensington, a housemaid to a merchant and, in 1881, a laundry maid to a solicitor.

The postcard that mentions the poorly baby was sent by Anthony and Mary's eldest daughter, Lily (b.1883). She was married to Charles *Ernest* Reeve (b.1879), a domestic coachman. He would later become a taxi cab driver. Lily was right to reassure her mother. Baby Frances lived until she was 91.

I was unable to trace who had sent the postcard to Daisy. The All Saints'

Convalescent Hospital in Eastbourne had a fierce reputation and in Kay Syrad's book *A Breath of Heaven*, an excerpt from the rules mentions: *Silence must be observed in the Wards after 8.30 p.m. and until 8 a.m. and always on the stairs and passages and at meals.* During the First World War the home was used by Canadian forces.

The three cards formed, I felt, a lovely story that connects the health concerns of our ancestors. It's also nice to keep a family's cards together.

Britain's first pillar box installed in Carlisle in 1853 – Various

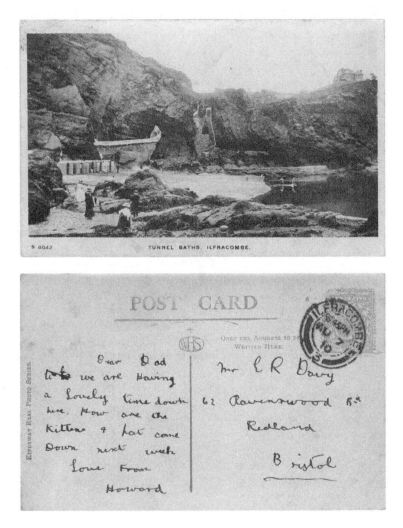

070013

070013
7 August 1910
62 Ravenswood Road
Redland
Bristol
Dear Dad
We are having a lovely time down here. How are the kittens and Pat. Come down next week.
Love from Howard.

Ernest Richard Davy (b.1858) lived in Ravenswood Road with his wife, Alice née Roberts (b.1867), and their son, Ernest *Howard* Davy (b.1900). Throughout the census returns, Ernest is listed as working for a corset maker. Alice was a school mistress and in 1939 she is listed as being a retired headmistress.

Her parents, William (b.1836) and Jane (b.1841) Roberts, were a clerk/foreman to a chemical works and the manageress of a fruit shop, respectively.

Is the card addressed just to the father because only the mother had gone on holiday – summer holidays from school? I imagine Pat was a cat, don't you?

Corset makers employed similar skills to tailoring and the items would be made to measure. Mass production allowed easier and more affordable garments to become available, moving the skills of the home-maker to the factory – Female Occupations, Margaret Ward

Humberstone Avenue, near Grimsby.

POST CARD.

THE ADDRESS ONLY TO BE
WRITTEN HERE.

THIS SPACE MAY BE USED
FOR COMMUNICATION.

Dear Frances just a PS to let
you know I am staying
again after all. They
promised to have someone
to help me a bit now. I
was down at Uncle George's
on Sunday to tea one of my
cousins is a married.

Miss Leary
c/o Miss Sharpley
Sheffield Manor
Market Rasen

071034

184

071034
11 March 1909
Miss Leary
C/O Miss Sharpley
Sheffield Manor
Market Rasen
Dear Jessie
Just a PC to let you know I am staying again after all. She has promised to have a woman to help me a bit more. I was down at Uncle George's at Grimsby to tea on Sunday. Wasn't I a marvel. Best love Hat.

I began with Jessie Leary (b.1884) and in 1911, she worked for a family headed by Annie Sharpley – a principal of a school.

Jessie was born in Thorseway, Lincolnshire and I found her in 1901 – aged 15 – working as a servant for a farmer in Grainthorpe.

In 1891, she was living with her parents, Robert (b.1844) a farm foreman and Charlotte née Baxter (b.1848). Also at home were Hannah (b.1881), Fanny (b.1883), James (b.1887) and Harriet (b.1888).

In 1939 Jessie was unmarried and living with her mother, Charlotte, and sister, Fanny.

Where was Harriet – who sent the card – in 1911? I found her working for John Hockney (b.1863) and his wife Sarah (b.1860) in Cleethorpes. John was a baker and confectioner.

In 1914, Jessie's eldest sister, Hannah, died. Hannah's husband was Charles Fell (b.1883), a boot repairer, and he married his sister-in-law, Hattie, in 1918.

Miss Sharpley was Annie Sharpley (b.1873). Her father was Anthony Sharpley (b.1837), a landowner. In 1891, her mother, Lucy (b.1840), was principal of Sheffield Manor Ladies School. In 1911, Annie is listed as the principal of a school. Her cousin, Jessie Sharpley (b.1850), is at the address as a housekeeper. Five girls aged from 12 to 16 are listed as boarders.

Who was Uncle George? I worked my way through Jessie's father's records, completing a list of his siblings. Robert had a brother called George (b.1851). However, Charlotte (née Baxter) also had a brother named George (b.1856). So, Uncle George was either George Leary or George Baxter. Both were alive in 1911. Both lived in Grimsby.

In Nature's Garden

That hills and valleys, dale and field,
And all the craggy mountains yield.

C. Marlowe.

POST CARD

NOTTINGHAM

7. ADDRESS ONLY

AUG 6 09

Dear Ma,
coming
home on Sunday
night time.
Colie.

Mrs G Broughton
54 Avenue Rd East
Clarendon Pk
Leicester

072099

With Loving
Birthday Wishes.

May Fortune never prove a jade,
And all your Fondest Hopes be paid;
If my wishes fruit could bear,
You'd be Rich beyond compare.

Windsor House
South Knighton Rd
Stoneygate
Dear Edie
        I am wishing
you many happy returns
of your 21st birthday
which is tomorrow
        I remains
            yours
        Annie.B.

Miss Edith Broughton
54 Avenue Rd
Clarendon Park
Local.

072099

187

072099
2 September 1911
57 Avenue Road
Clarendon Park
Leicester
Dear Edith
I am wishing you many happy returns of your 21st birthday, which is tomorrow.
I remain yours
Annie B
Windsor House
South Knighton Road
Stonygate

Dear Ma
Home on Sunday night.
Love Edie

Edith Broughton was born in 1891, the youngest of 12 children born to her parents, George (b.1846) and Eliza née Wells (b.1849). In 1911, Edith lived with her parents and one brother, Isaac (b.1889). Her father is listed as a bricklayer with Midland Railway and Edith as a hosiery machinist in a warehouse. Isaac was a carpenter.

As soon as I began creating Edith's family tree, I was being prompted to a high number of Ancestry hints. I only explore the information in the trees created by others when I am certain I have the foundations of my research in place. Once I had completed my usual checks I explored what others had found. I already had that Edith married James Pickford (b.1867) in 1918 and the first tree I reviewed confirmed this and also provided me with the few missing siblings that I hadn't yet traced – I now had 12, and 12 was the number declared in the 1911 census. I was also able to confirm that Edith and James Pickford had one child. Norman was born in 1918. In 1929, I found James and Norman as first-class passengers sailing to England from South Africa. James's occupation is listed as a hosiery manufacturer. James also appears in several trade directories as a fancy hosiery manufacturer.

I found James and Norman again in 1943. Norman's probate records mention that he 'died 22 August 1943 on war service'. At this time James is a director of a company. Norman's grave is in County Fermanagh and he was a flight sergeant in the RAF. The FindAGrave website lists him as a navigator and has a summary of how Norman was killed:

201 Squadron was based at RAF Castle Archdale, Irvinestown, Co. Fermanagh, from where it flew 'Flying Boats', principally the Short Sunderland, over the North Atlantic in support of shipping convoys, and also to seek German submarines... [the plane] crashed into the lower slopes of Mount Brandon, Co. Kerry, at 06.00 on the morning of 22 August 1943. Of the 11 men on board the aircraft, 8 were killed.

It wasn't until I found James and Norman in the passenger list in 1929 that I had an indication of James's birth year. That led me to him in the 1939 register where he is listed as a widower and retired hosiery manufacturer.

Edith had died in 1918. Within a few months of her marriage and the birth of her child she died from pneumonia – just days before Norman's first Christmas.

One of the trees I reviewed had a photo of Edith. Dressed in a winter coat, she stands with a fur muffler and scarf. I would imagine she was in her twenties when the photograph was taken – perhaps just after her 21st birthday. It often doesn't take long to trace a person's life. In Edith's case it was a short one

I found very little information about James. Most of what I discovered connects him to Edith and their son. Even the other family trees that include Edith and the lovely photo of her don't have anything more. They had even less than I had. This story needed more information to answer my questions and I decided to order Edith and James's marriage certificate and that proved to be a good investment as it showed that James was a widower. With that information I worked back, trying to find a previous marriage and then the death of that wife. I actually discovered that James had been married twice before.

His first wife was Zilpah Osborne (b.1863) and she was born in Staffordshire. Her parents were Daniel (b.1822) and Ann Osborne (b.1828). Daniel was a silk twister. Ann and two of Zilpah's sisters were silk winders. Zilpah married James Pickford in 1891 and they had three children: Alice (b.1893), William (b.1895) and Elsie (b.1897). Zilpah died in 1901.

James's second wife was Lucy Jefferies (b.1871) and they married in 1907. In 1911, James and Lucy were living with his children in Staffordshire. Lucy died in 1912.

I was now able to trace James via census returns. His parents were William (b.1844) and Mary Pickford (b.1843). William was a manager in a silk mill and later became a silk manufacturer. In 1881, James was a warehouse lad. In 1901, the widowed James and his children lived with his parents.

Even though I often have more than one card for a story, I don't include those extras unless they add to the story. In Edith's case, having a card sent to and from her, seeing her handwriting, does add to Edith's story. I'd always considered that Edith's short life was a sad tale, but once I knew James's story, his is equally so – he married three times and all three wives died young.

Finding he had three other children, apart from Norman who was killed during the Second World War, added some light to the picture.

Who sent the card? Well, I had the address and the card was signed 'Annie B'. A quick search found a Broughton family living in the road. Leonard (b.1867) was Edith's eldest brother, born in 1867. He and his wife, Annie (b.1867), had seven children. I thought it strange that the sender of the card – Annie – hadn't mentioned her husband and children when wishing Edith a happy birthday – there's even a sense of formality. Perhaps Leonard – 24 years older than his sister – had little contact even though they lived just over a mile away.

The first factory to produce hosiery opened in Leicester in 1855 – Female Occupations, Margaret Ward

073090

073090
1912
Mrs Neilson
42 Paget Rd
Leicester
England
XXXX
Dear Mamma
Just Pcard to let you know I will not be home tomorrow morning as we would have to change and arrive about 3 o'clock in morning, so we will be coming for sure on Saturday night. I will write a Pcard to let you know what time we arrive. I hope you will get this tomorrow as I thought Uncle John had written I am staying for two or three days in Rutherglen and that's how I did not know till he came and told me he had not [?] as made [?] I knew.
Yours Ada

Although the ink on the postcard had suffered from smudging, the family tree confirmed that the card was sent from Ada Neilson (b.1899) to her mother Anna née Shaw (b.1878).

In 1911, the family lived at Paget Road and James Neilson (b.1876) worked as a stereotyper in the printing industry.

James and Anna had five children: Ada, Amy (b.1902), Catherine (b.1905), John (b.1907) and George (b.1910).

Ada had been staying with her family in Glasgow and Uncle John (b.1878) was a printer's compositor. Another brother, Archibald Neilson (b.1884), was a joiner's apprentice. In 1911, I found American emigration records matching Archibald. He arrived in Massachusetts and settled there. He married Agnes (b.1885) and the couple had a daughter, Catherine (b.1914). It was difficult to confirm categorically that this was the correct Archibald. However, the only Archibald born in the same date range in Scotland was a doctor. All of the American records show Archibald as a carpenter.

Ada's paternal grandfather, John Neilson (b.1853), also worked in the printing trade. In 1901, he is listed as a letter press printer. Ada's grandmother, Catherine née Walker (b.1855), was born in Bute and her family were mainly weavers. In 1891, Catherine's sister, Flora (b.1860), is recorded as a power loom weaver. In 1901, another sister, Elizabeth (b.1870), worked in a steam laundry.

It's ironic, given Ada's father, uncle and grandfather's industry, that the card is so badly smudged.

POST CARD.

13 B For INLAND Postage only this space may
be used for communication.

The ADDRESS only to be written here.

Should like to hear
how you are I only
got back last week —
will tell you more when
I write again I hope
your dear Sisters are
well also yourself
E Cook

Miss E Stevens
19 Sydney Terrace
Dorchester

074011

074011
25 September 1905
Miss C Stevens
19 Sydney Terrace
Dorchester
Should like to hear how you are. I only got back last week – will tell you more when I write
again. I hope your dear sisters are well and yourself.
C Pook

Caroline was born in Melbury Osmond, Dorset. She was baptised in December 1839 and her parents were William (b.1793) and Caroline née Clinch (b.1806). William was a labourer. The couple had at least six other children: William (b.1827), Thomas (b.1830), Mary (b.1833), Emma (b.1835), Eliza (b.1843) and Samuel (b.1847).

In 1911, Caroline is listed at the address on the card living with her widowed sister, Emma Stevens. Emma has added more information than was required – including their dates and places of birth. I am happy that Emma and Caroline are sisters but I was unable to trace Emma's marriage – perhaps to another Stevens. There are many to choose from so I cannot include the details without more evidence to support the result. Caroline is listed as a retired servant. She died 11 years later and the address given was Sydney Terrace.

In 1901, Mary is shown in the census return as a nurse living with the son of her brother William in Surrey. William (b.1866) junior's family lived in a lodge, perhaps part of the estate of William Grant (b.1853) who was born in India and is recorded as an indigo planter. William Grant died in the Grand Hotel, Cannes in 1923. William's first son was Gregor Grant (b.1880) and he died in India in 1919.

Novelist Anthony Trollope worked in the postal service for 33 years and was responsible for trialing posting boxes in the Channel Islands – Various

075083

195

075083
1911
Miss Carrie Openshaw
21 Red Bank Road
Radcliff
Nr Manchester
With Love
Eunice

In 1911, Carrie's mother, Caroline née Leyland (b.1853), was a widow and despite this she had included in the census return that she'd had eight children and one had died: Mary (b.1875), Margaret (b.1876), Lilly (b.1878), Clara (b.1881), Bertha (b.1883), Arthur (b.1886), Walter (b.1888), Carrie (b.1890). Their father, Robert (b.1853), was a coalminer and had died in 1894.

Carrie married Wilfred Lord (b.1890) in 1915. At this time she was a cotton weaver and he was a grocer's assistant. By 1939 the couple had moved to Blackpool and Wilfred was an insurance agent. His father, James (b.1865), had been a stonemason and by 1911, Wilfred's widowed mother, Emily née Hilton (b.1863), ran an off-licence.

Three of Carrie's sisters also moved to Blackpool. Margaret, Lily and Clara are listed as working as company house-keepers – possibly running their own boarding house.

Caroline née Leyland, Carrie's mother, was the daughter of a cotton weaver. Many of her children would also work as weavers – including Carrie. The family lived in an industrial area. In 1901, their neighbours were also weavers. Some manufactured clogs and another neighbour was a colliery foreman.

"WON'T YOU GIVE ME A KISS, DEAR?"
"THE IDEA! WHAT CHEEK!
OH! I PREFER THE LIPS!"

076069

076069
1911
Mr J Palmer
L. Benefield
Oundle
Oh if this was only you

I found Edmund John Palmer (b.1889) living with his parents, William
(b.1843) and Elizabeth née Gilby (b.1845), and sister Susanna (b.1880). He
had been listed in the 1911 census as John and outside of the column, his
father had added Edmund – clearly suggesting that he was known by his
middle name.

Including John and his sister, the couple had eight children: Frank
(b.1868), William (b.1870), Sarah (b.1873), Fanny (b.1875), Bertram (b.1878),
Susanna (b.1880), Victoria (b.1888) and Edmund John (b.1889).

In 1911, William was a shepherd and John is listed as a farm labourer. In
earlier census returns I found the father's occupation as a woodman and
baker – and this was confirmed on at least one marriage document.

In 1911, Frank was a gardener, living with his wife, Elizabeth née Vessey
(b.1868), in Northamptonshire. By 1911, William was a widower and his
sister, Victoria, worked for him as his housekeeper. At this time he was
working as a woodman.

Not all the children stayed close to home. In 1891, Sarah worked as a
servant in the Greyhound Hotel, Lea Bridge Road, Leyton. Fanny worked as
a servant in Brighton. In 1901, Bertram was a servant in Cherington,
Gloucestershire working for a vicar.

John's mother's family had interesting jobs. Elizabeth Gilby had at least
seven siblings. Fanny (b.1843) and Sarah Gilby (b.1846) worked as maids –
Fanny working for a vicar in Longdon, Staffordshire, and Sarah working for a
magistrate in Welwyn, Hertfordshire. Edmund (b.1848) was a gardener and
lived in Northamptonshire. John (b.1852) worked in London as a butler and
his death was registered in 1917 in Kensington.

Once I reached that generation and had confirmed the parents, the tree
opened up and Ancestry led me to other trees. I was able to trace Elizabeth's
mother, Fanny née Pywell (b.1816), and father, Francis Gilby (b.1816). I'm
never keen to go too far back without corroborating the information but two
of the trees I looked at had completed extensive research. I haven't checked it
and I only present the information because it links to the family on the
postcard. Fanny's father was Duke Pywell (b.1775) and the fascinating fact to
me about this man is that he was a shepherd – directly linking through his
occupation to William Palmer's. Incredibly, the family's tree has been
researched back to 1601 and the birth of John Pywell – Duke's great-great-
great-grandfather. The research was supported by scanned images of source

documents.

Having an overview of the family is such a bonus – apart from Duke's connection to future generations through their work, it's lovely to see that the family brings into future generations the name of a loved one: grandmother Fanny née Pywell (b.1816), mother Fanny née Gilby (b.1843) and daughter Fanny Palmer (b.1875).

What of John? He married Florence née Bird (b.1889) in 1917 and he served in the First World War with the Royal Engineers. In 1939 he was a general gardener for a public school. Who sent the card? Unfortunately I was unable to match the handwriting to Florence's – but I like to think it was from her, because that might explain why he (possibly) kept it and in such good condition.

Watts Park, Southampton.

077106
21 August 1911
Mrs Leesing
Grange View
Walkeringham
Gainsbro'
Dear S
I daresay you will know why I have not come. I am still at home & can't get a train to come back yet. I will let you know when I am coming though. Isn't this strike dreadful. Shall be glad when it is over. I am writing to Joe by this post so he will tell you all the news. Love to all.
Florrie.

Sarah Leesing née Woodhead (b.1877) lived at the address with her husband, Albert Leesing (b.1882), a labourer in a brickyard. They had married in 1908. In 1911, Sarah's father, John Woodhead (b.1838), was listed as a retired innkeeper. Further back, the family appear at the Brickmaker's Arms in Walkeringham. Earlier, John was a grocer. Sarah had at least five siblings, including a half-brother, John Cobb (b.1865), from her mother Hannah's first marriage. Hannah née Thursby's first husband was John Cobb (b.1839) and he died in in 1867.

The postcard mentions Joe and that is most likely to be Sarah's other brother – recorded as Joseph (b.1880). In 1911, he was living with his parents and worked as a labourer. I wasn't able to trace a Florrie or a Florence. Joseph died without marrying in 1929. In 1939, Albert, Sarah's husband, still worked as a labourer and was also a special constable.

With Albert being employed in a brickyard and Sarah's family running a pub named the Brickmaker's Arms, it's no surprise to learn that brickmaking was a prominent industry in and around Walkeringham. As ever, I found some very informative blogs created by local historians. In particular, East Midland Named Bricks was very detailed. The area produced distinctive white bricks – as well as the more traditional red. If you're interested in brickmaking, do have a look at the blog. The article I read was uploaded in 2016 and there were no comments – such a shame for all that work not to be acknowledged. The site's still active – my comment was reviewed and published within seconds.

My father spent many years making bricks and I have memories of visiting the once independent Swanage Brick and Tile Co. I can still smell its distinctive scent – a mix of sand and clay, especially when the kilns were fired.

Florrie mentions a strike in her message and this is a reference to the first national rail strike. Workers were striking in an attempt to bring about better wages and working conditions. The strike led to six deaths – in the Llanelli Riots. Troops had been sent to clear a blockade and strikers and spectators were involved with clashes with the army. Apart from those few details I found very little about the strike. Searches in library databases and online were relatively unsuccessful. Again, it was a blog that carried the most information.

The Turnip Rail blog had 'The Forgotten National Rail Strike, 1911' – a three-part series written by Dr David Turner. The articles include very detailed research, written by David in 2010. If you'd like to learn more about the strike – that ultimately led to the formation of the National Union of Railwaymen – I'd recommend you visit his blog.

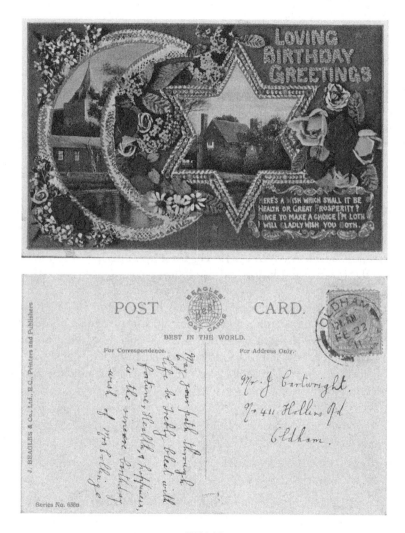

078017

078017
22 February 1911
Mr J Cartwright
No 411 Hollins Road
Oldham
May your path through life be trebly blest with fortune, health and happiness, is the sincere birthday wish of Mrs Collinge.

James Cartwright was born in 1829 in Lancashire. In 1911, just after the postcard was sent, James was a widower living at the address as a boarder. However, the Cartwright family can be traced to 409–411 Hollins Road to at least 1871. James's wife was Mary née Welsh (b.1830) and she had died in 1908.

In the various census returns, James's occupation is listed as a furniture broker. In 1861, he was working in a cotton mill and the family lived at Copster Hill. James and Mary had at least seven children.

Joshua (b.1851) was a grocer's carter and later a coalminer. He and his wife Agnes had nine children; three had died by 1911.

Emma (b.1858) married John Taylor, a horse keeper in a colliery.

Ann (b.1860) married Thomas Jagger. The couple emigrated to Canada with their children and she died there in 1928. Thomas was a watchman.

Sarah (b.1864) married Walter Leech, a hardware dealer, and in 1911 he is listed as the head of the household in Hollins Road. Walter and Sarah were still there in 1939.

I felt a little sorry for James. For decades he'd lived in Hollins Road – at least from 1871 – as a father, grandfather, and head of the household. In 1911, he wasn't even listed as father-in-law – just boarder. The probate records from 1911 show James's address as Hollins Road.

I was unable to trace Mrs Collinge. There were many candidates and some even lived in Hollins Road.

"Miles' Clock Tower, Exeter"

SOUVENIR POST CARD

Valentine's Series
Printed in Great Britain.

Dear Annie just a line to
tell you that I got here alright
about 11.30. after a long journey
train did not stop at
Exeter so they took me on
to Dawlish there was several
of us took back again only
we was soon back again only
there was at the station to meet me
I spent one own Eoie on clock
long without mellow with love
to all

Mrs A Summers
Gas Works
Chew Magna
Nr Bristol

079063

079063
23 September 1912
Gas Works
Chew Magna
Near Bristol
Dear Annie
Just a line to tell you that I got here alright about 1.30 after a long journey. Train did not stop at Exeter so they took me on to Dawlish. There was several of us but I did not mind. We was soon back again. Mother & Millie was at the station to meet me. I went and seen Edie. She is looking fine. George is about the same and mother love to all.

Annie Summers (b.1875) lived at the gas works with her husband Edward (b.1873) – the manager of the gas works – and their children: Reginald (b.1896) who was a domestic gardener, Mabel (b.1899) and Wilfred (b.1902). Annie was born in Exeter, Edward in Wales, and the children were born in Somerset.

When I revisited the tree after my initial research, I discovered that the information added for 1901 could possibly be incorrect. I had the family as living in Brislington. All the names and ages were correct. However, Edward was listed as being from Wells, Somerset. I decided to delete everything apart from the 1911 information and begin again. Family trees are like ill-fitting shoes. You want them to fit, but sometimes you have to admit that the pain of forcing something just isn't worth it.

I decided to focus on the children – a new search on Reginald took me straight to that Brislington family. The only difference I discovered was that Mabel was *Florence* Mabel. I searched for her birth and confirmed she was Florence – and updated the tree accordingly. I found Reginald in 1939 working as a gas service layer. I still had the confusion of Wells and Wales. Although I traced the couple's marriage in 1895, there was no image available that might confirm his place of birth. However, it did confirm his father's name – Edward (b.1836). I believe I found the family in 1881, living in Nailsea. Edward senior is listed as a miner. Edward junior... born in Wales. Perhaps the recorder in 1901 misheard Edward and assumed he meant Wells. After all, it's unlikely he would have had a Welsh accent.

Annie was also difficult to trace. I had her as Annie Elizabeth and all my searches came back with Elizabeth Annie. However, she is Annie Elizabeth in the marriage records.

This should have been a relatively straightforward research project – yet it seemed impossible to confirm anything beyond each separate document.

Sometimes we can't see the wood for the trees – a cliché so apt for this particular story. I returned to the 1911 census to check whether Edward's writing of Wales could have been transcribed incorrectly. No, it was very clear. Then I spotted Reginald's place of birth: Brislington. I'd spent so much energy on the Wells/Wales issue I'd missed this important detail. Therefore, as far I could prove, the Brislington connection was correct. Edward's place of birth in the 1901 census was incorrect.

The card mentions Mother, Millie, Edie and George – perhaps Annie's siblings. But who is the card from? I found Elizabeth Annie Noble in 1881 – living with her family in Exeter. One of her sisters was Florence – which might connect to the daughter.

Old Mill at Ambleside

080084

080084
3 February 1914
Mrs Ernest Cheffey
Tincleton
Nr Dorchester
Dorset
Dearest Ciss & E
Many thanks for your very nice card. I have been so busy I've not had a bit of time to write lately but I expect you heard from Mam that we still got a lodger and it's a good bit to do but it's better weather now and dry. Love to you both from us all.
Dolly is a big girl and she asks where is Ian.
From Dolly to Auntie
XXXXXXXXX

I was looking forward to researching this card. Tincleton isn't too far from where I live in Dorset and I hoped some of the other locations would be familiar to me. I even went to school with a girl named Cheffey – but that's another story.

Ernest Cheffey (b.1884) lived in Tincleton with his family. In 1911, he was an auxiliary postman.

George (b.1856) and Ellen née House (b.1857) had eight children including Ernest: Arthur (b.1879), Florence (b.1884), Ernest, Bertram (b.1888), Ada (b.1890), Minnie (b.1893), Caroline (b.1894) and Elsie (b.1898). At this time George and Arthur were farm workers.

In 1911, Minnie worked as a servant in Devon. Caroline had left home and was in Tincleton working for Emma Pollard (b.1869) who ran a laundry.

Ernest married Hester née Riggs (b.1886) in 1913. In 1911, she was a servant working for John Gravener and his family in Dorchester. Gravener was a retired Royal Navy captain. The very grand Avenue House is now a dental practice. Hester's birth is registered to Bockhampton – famous for being the birthplace of Thomas Hardy (b.1840). In census returns the family lived in nearby Stinsford, near to the church where Hardy's heart is buried in its grounds.

Hester had five siblings: George (b.1884), Annie (b.1888), Arthur (b.1890), William (b.1895) and Frederick (b.1900).

Hester's mother, Annie Riggs née Bowles (b.1864), was born in Cerne Abbas. Her parents are listed as John (b.1824) and Esther Bowles (b.1828) and the family lived in Acreman Street.

Ernest's sister, Florence Cheffey, married George Riggs – a brother of Hester's.

With so many locations associated with Thomas Hardy – both as family homes and as places used in his work – I wondered where his family might have lived in relation to the ones in this tree. I began, as always, with the 1911 census and found Thomas Hardy living in Dorchester. There were no surprises there, but it was lovely to see that the return was in his own handwriting – and that his occupation was author of books.

Of course, I could have read any one of hundreds of online summaries of Hardy's life, but I continued with the family's tree. His baptism records confirm that his father, Thomas, was a mason. In the register for Hardy's second marriage, his father is recorded as a builder. In 1851, the father was a bricklayer. In 1871, Thomas is listed as an architect's clerk.

As I've mentioned elsewhere, extracting information from the various census returns and registers can only tell part of a person's story. Hardy's tree doesn't tell me that he lived for a short time in the town where I now live. So much of life falls between those 10-year snapshots, and if you intend researching your own tree, keep an open mind to what you discover and what you may have missed.

Unfortunately, I didn't discover a more precise location that connects Hardy to the Cheffey family. However, the Bockhampton and Stinsford areas are relatively remote and it's almost certain that the families would be known to each other.

Throughout the searches I found a conflict between Cheffey and Chaffey. However, using Tincleton as the anchor I believe I followed the correct branches of this tree.

Who sent the card? Both Ernest and Hester had large families. I failed to find a Dolly or a name that could have become Dolly.

The Queen's Cottage, Kew.

Mrs J. Lewis.
Grove Villa
Queens Rd
Stonehouse

081076

211

081076
5 July 1912
Mr J Lewis
Grove Villa
Queens Road
Stonehouse
Dear M & F
Hope to see you on Sunday, shall come by afternoon train.
Have been offered Brimscombe West.
Hope you are A1.
With love
Jim

Joseph (b.1854) and Eliza Lewis (b.1852) lived in Queens Road, Stonehouse. Joseph was a railway signalman and the couple had eight children. Their eldest son, Charles (b.1877), was a railway clerk. Another son, Harvey (b.1879), appears in railway employment records from the age of 15 as a lad porter and later as a signal porter. In 1897 he was punished for 'coming late on duty, also for not properly attending to the shunting of a horse box, whereby it was damaged'. By the 1930s, when he sailed with his wife Mary to Canada, he was listed as a secretary. Francis Lewis (b.1881) was listed in 1901 as a solicitors' clerk – possibly one of the few sons not to enter into railway employment.

Who sent the card? Frederick *James* (b.1887) most certainly did work for the railways. In 1911, he was a signalman in Wales. By 1939 he had returned to Gloucestershire with his family, still working as a signalman. But he returned much earlier than that – the postcard was sent in Gloucestershire and refers to Brimscombe West, a signal box junction.

You might recognise the address on this postcard – Gilbert Freeman's family (from the first story in this book) lived in Queens Road. Although they weren't neighbours, the families may have been known to each other.

ORIENT-ROYAL MAIL LINE S.S. OROTAVA
AT NAPLES

Nov. 11th 1910

POST CARD.

This space to be used for Correspondence only.

The Address only to be written here

THE ORIENT-ROYAL MAIL LINE

LONDON
NOV 12 00
AM

How do you feel about a
mixed match v Repton
this year on Dec. 27th? I am
awfully keen on it myself. What about a
side something like this, J.C. Felt in
goal. Backs yourself + I.M. Hett
halves Rhodes, Per. J. N. N. W. (if he will
play + Molly Powell. Bernard
Hoskins centre forward L.K. Hett
a some girl on one wing A.I. Hett
a some girl on the other. I don't see
why we should not give them a
game. Not on Boxing-day of course
but 27th Dec. Perhaps you will
be bringing a gal (in lieu of Rhodes
who would not want to play)
Drop me a line re this A. (too busy)

H. E. Bowden Esq
19, Derrington Avenue
Crewe

082031

213

082031
11 November 1910
HE Bowden Esquire
19 Durrington Avenue
Crewe
How do you feel about a mixed match v Reigate this year on <u>Dec 27th.</u> I am awfully keen
on it myself. What about a side something like this:
HC Hett in goal
Backs yourself and IM Hett
Halves Rhodes, Rev JHMW (if he will play) and Molly Powell
Bernard Hoskins centre forward
LK Hett & some girl on one wing
AI Hett and some girl on the other
I don't see why we should not give them a game.
Not on Boxing Day of course but 27th Dec.
Perhaps you will be bringing a pal in lieu of Rhodes who would not <u>want</u> to play drop me a
line re this.
AI Hett

The sender of this postcard certainly got his halfpenny's worth out of the postal system!

In 1911, Herbert Bowden (b1891) was listed at the address as a lodger. The only other person recorded was a visitor, his mother, Mary née Hampton (b.1856). At this time, Herbert was a premium apprentice with a locomotives works.

Mary was Herbert's father's second wife. The Reverend James Bowden's (b.1835) first wife was Mary née Trenchard and the couple had at least five children.

Mary née Hampton was the daughter of a merchant. Charles Hampton is listed in various roles, including being a Manchester agent – a broker for goods manufactured in Manchester. He's also listed as working as an agent for the West India Co.

Herbert was the only child of James and Mary. In 1901, he lived with his parents and half-siblings in Sussex. In 1910 he is shown working for the London and North Western Railway Company in the locomotive department.

In 1914 Herbert appears in a passenger list arriving in America. He settled for a while in Canada and in 1915 enlisted in the Canadian Army. At that time his employment was letter carrier. He eventually returned to England with his wife, Adele née Martin, and their children.

It was impossible to unravel the exact details of the names mentioned on the postcard – what a planner the sender was!

Canal:
Plan No. 2.

CANAL MARITIME DE SUEZ

Post card. Postkarte. Carte postale.
Dopisnice. Correspondenzkarte. Brefkort.
Всемірный почтовый союзъ. Россія. Открытое письмо.
Karta korespondencyjna. Korespondenční lístek.

ONE PENNY

Mr. A. Samson.
24 Northumberland R[?]
Nichols Town
Southampton
Hants
England

083094

215

083094
16 November 1911
Mr A Samson
24 Northumberland Road
Southampton
Hants England
HMS Royal Arthur
My dear chum.
As you can tell by this PC we have arrived in safe we called ship yesterday. Leave here tomorrow. I am going ashore this afternoon but on patrol (work) it is scorching hot here. Hope all are well your old mate Charles.
Received your letters and paper safe.

Arthur Samson (b.1888) lived with his widowed mother, Jane Samson née Fergusson (b.1858), and siblings, Benjamin (b.1884), Jane (b.1886), Eva (b.1891), Margaret (b.1894) and Constance (b.1897). Benjamin and Arthur worked in the docks and both became foremen. Jane was a cook and Eva a housekeeper. Arthur married Doris née Brewer (b.1898). Her father, Charles Brewer (b.1867), was a roller man in a flour mill.

Arthur's father, Benjamin Haffenden Samson (b.1856), was a letterpress printer and he died in 1908. Benjamin had at least five siblings and their names are intriguing: John Martin, Mary Austen, Henry Rofe, Elizabeth Adams and Haffenden Stephen.

Their mother was Margaret née Martin (b.1817) – which explains John's middle name. But what about the others? I explored other trees for this family, but they had less information than I had discovered. Relying solely on online searches for the early 19th century is not recommended and I decided to leave this family's earlier story for another time.

The tradition of names was carried into Arthur's generation. His middle name was Martin, his sister Jane's middle name was Austen and his brother Benjamin's middle name was Fergusson – their mother's maiden name.

Jane Fergusson was the daughter of an engraver, John Fergusson (b.1856). As I searched further back I discovered a Jane Fergusson living with an uncle and aunt in 1881 – Freeman (b.1809) and Ann Harsant (b.1808). I hadn't seen that surname before so I created their tree to see if I could confirm this was the correct Jane. Also living at the address was Ellen Harsant (b.1867), granddaughter, and recorded as orphan. Ann Freeman's maiden name was Whislay and she was the sister of Jane's mother, Lucy née Whislay (b.1836). Ellen's father was William Harsant (b.1839) and he had died in 1868 – a year after Ellen's birth.

There are so many branches to this tree and I know that each one carries a story – I'm always reluctant to stop searching because I know I'm perhaps only a click away from a revelation. I would like to know how Ellen had been orphaned – but she's not close enough to the postcard to continue searching.

If you look at some trees that are available online, it's actually very difficult – if not impossible – to track their connections. Knowing when to stop is often something we learn the hard way.

I wish I knew who had sent the postcard to Arthur. Clearly they were good friends. I know the ship had sailed from Portsmouth – but apart from finding several seamen with the first name Charles, I was unable to confirm who this Charles actually was.

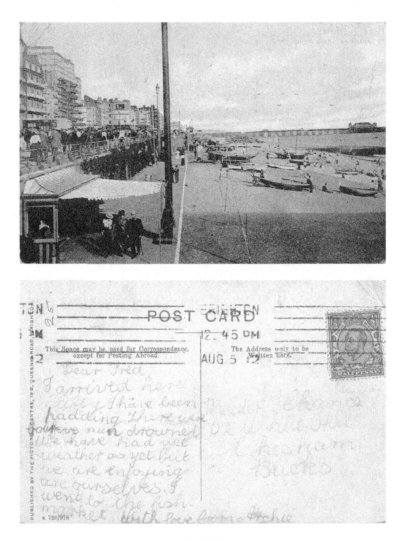

084095

084095
5 August 1912
Master F Charles
52 White Hill
Chesham
Bucks
Dear Fred
I arrived here safely. I have been paddling. There were ~~five~~ four men drowned. We have had
wet weather as yet but we are enjoying ~~are~~ ourselves. I went to the fish market.
With love from Archie.

Although the postcard was addressed to number 52, Fred (b.1903) and his family lived at number 54. His parents were Thomas (b.1870) and Edith née Reynolds (b.1872). Thomas was a boot riveter in a factory. Edwin Newton (b.1850), who lived next door in number 52, was a self-employed bootmaker, working from home. Next door, on the other side, at number 56, lived John Dickinson (b.1840), a retired boot checker. Chesham museum has a wonderful website with photographs of the area's history – including images of workers in factories where boots and shoes were made. The area's also known for the manufacture of brushes and barrels.

Fred Chance had five siblings and by 1911 one had died – Edith (b.1896), Ethel (b.1898), Hilda (b.1907) and David (b.1909).

William Chance (b.1844), Fred's paternal grandfather, was a shoemaker. His grandmother, Emily née Lewis (b.1848), was a dressmaker. John Reynolds (b.1836), Fred's maternal grandfather, was a carpenter. His maternal grandmother, Caroline née Mayo (b.1837), was the daughter of a butcher. In the 1861 census, the family's trades include a shoe binder (the adding of wax to waterproof the gap between sole, upper and heel). Neighbours also worked in the shoe industry and brush-making.

I discovered a lovely photograph on the My Brighton and Hove website of Brighton's fish market. The image is dated between 1900 and 1914 and the caption refers to the crowds watching from the promenade – just as Archie may have done.

Of course, the most shocking part of Archie's message is about the loss of life. Who were the men? I was able to find several newspaper reports about the incident – the tragedy was even reported in America. A blog post written several years ago provided more information.

Dave Curran had written about Caius House in Battersea, which he passed on a regular commute when he lived in the area. The following excerpt is from Dave's blog:

Caius House housed an assortment of clubs and activities… [Historic Building recording and Field Evaluation in 2008] The most impressive feature of the building was a stained glass window… It has been identified as a design by Sir Edward Burne-Jones by the V & A Museum… This window commemorates the lives of four young men who died tragically in a drowning accident in Saltdean in August 1912 while the Caius Summer Club was in session… Lady Georgiana Burne-Jones had a home in Rottingdean and, upset by the tragedy, offered to release a Burne-Jones memorial window to the memory of the four boys.

The building was eventually demolished – although the window was removed and it was intended to reinstate it in the replacement. However, I still hadn't managed to discover the names of the four young men – or any more details. When I returned to this story after a break of a few months, I found additional information that included the names of the four victims. Tony Sanders, a director in Caius House in 2015, posted in the forum British-Genealogy.com a response to an earlier query and mentioned that 'We have a window that commemorates the lives of four young men… this is on loan to Gonville and Caius College, Cambridge and we are in the process of having a copy made ready to install'.

Another post in the forum shared this: 'The names in the stained glass are George Henry Allen, Frederick Beford, Conrad Thomas Ancrum Betts and Frederick John Taylor. They were all aged about 20 at the time'.

From that information I was able to trace three of the four men and believe I possibly found the fourth:

George was a machine and tool designer and the son of a motor engineer. Frederick was an assurance clerk and the son of a coachbuilder. Conrad was an iron worker and the son of a carpenter and joiner. There were several Frederick Taylors in the area, but I am relatively content that I have the correct man and he was a clerk and the son of a restaurant worker.

Who was Archie? Well, I assumed that he must live relatively close to Fred. It didn't take long to discover an Archibald Thorn (b.1902) living at number 62 – in the same road to Fred. Archie's father, Albert Thorn (b.1874), was – no surprises here – a boot riveter.

085020

085020
13 March 1910
FE Fermor, Esq
Virginia Villa, 106 Whitley Road
Eastbourne
Had a very comfortable journey home last night without any rain and without leaving anything behind I think! Have just been looking [?] the [?] of the parcel which [?] very interesting.
Mother's cold is rather bad today but [?] is be here [?] not a little busy.
I hope Mrs Fermor is better. All my love and many thanks to all for the very pleasant time yesterday
From R.

Frank Edgar Fermor was born in Hastings in 1872. He lived there for a number of years with his parents, Frederick C Fermor (b.1847) and Ellen née Baggs (b.1850), and siblings, Edith (b.1875) and Arthur (b.1879).

In 1891, Frank was a shorthand clerk, living with his parents and siblings in Station Road, Hastings. By 1911, he had moved to Eastbourne, and was living with his wife of less than one year and employed as an accountant.

Although his mother does not appear in the 1911 census with her son, it's clear from the postcard message that she must live nearby – and she is also in Eastbourne, living with Edith. Her status is widow.

In 1901, Frederick Fermor is a boarder in Bermondsey, London, working as a clerk. I reviewed some other family trees and they all had Frederick as being alive in 1911 – in fact, they had him dying in 1914. I initially decided that I had followed the wrong Frederick to London and that he must have died before 1911.

The Bermondsey Frederick was born in Hastings – as was Frank's father. I needed to trace the death – or deaths – of both Frederick Fermors. I found only one that fitted the age at death: Frederick C Fermor and he died 1914 in Bermondsey.

If he didn't die until 1914, where was he in 1911? In Bermondsey, that's where! He was working as a commercial clerk and living as a boarder. The head of the household has, very conveniently, added that he is married and has three children – this is then struck out.

Had Frank's parents separated and lived apart for long enough for no one in Eastbourne to know the truth – or at least anyone involved with the census returns? It wasn't unknown for this kind of deliberate error to be made.

Who sent the card? The answer is in the 1911 census. The message on the postcard is affectionate and, I feel, bubbling with excitement. It's signed 'R'.

In 1910, Frank married Rosa née Watson (b.1873). In 1911, Rosa's mother, Charlotte (b.1845), has her status in the census as married, changed to widowed – it seems that both mothers conspired to confuse me!

The Rumbling Bridge
Dunkeld.

POST CARD.

THIS SPACE MAY BE USED
FOR CORRESPONDENCE
FOR INLAND ONLY

ADDRESS TO BE WRITTEN HERE

Miss Florence Hawley
"Winslow"
Bucks

086050

086050

5 January 1908
Miss Florence Hawley
Winslow
Bucks

Many thanks for your letters. This morning's news has delighted me. Am now eagerly looking forward to seeing you.
Will write to you for Wednesday morning at Penarth.
Fondest love. Bea.

Before Florence Hawley (b.1881) married Christopher Shapland (b.1881) in 1913, she was a governess working for a mining engineer in Derbyshire. Christopher's father, Charles Shapland (b.1847), was a jeweller. Christopher was a clerk in holy orders. Florence and Christopher would later live in the rectory at Norton-sub-Hamdon in Somerset. Christopher's brother, Thomas (b.1879), was a silversmith and dealer.

In 1911, three years after the postcard had been sent, Florence lived with her family in Winslow. James Hawley (b.1851) was a grocer and provisions dealer. Susan née Perkins (b.1857) was the daughter of a chemist. In a photograph taken of the premises in the early years of the 20th century, an awning outside the family business declares 'JC Hawley established 1761'. However, in the couple's marriage register of 1879, James's father – also James (b.1805) – is listed as a farmer.

Delving back into earlier records I found James senior listed as a grocer *and* farmer of 218 acres. A trade directory from 1786 states that the business also included a workshop and stable, and traded as a grocer and tallow chandler. In the following decade Hawley also traded in ironmongery. The premises are substantial and it's no surprise to see in the various census returns that several of the shop employees live in the accommodation with the family.

In 1901, Florence's sister, Edith (b.1884), was a pupil at Beethoven House in Northamptonshire – a music school run by accomplished organist Brook Sampson. Adverts declare it to be a 'high class school for girls'. As well as teaching, Sampson would give concerts in the town hall. He was also a published author. Edith married James Johnstone (b.1889), an auctioneer.

Leslie (b.1888), Florence and Edith's brother, worked in the shop and was still there in 1939 as a grocer and wine merchant. Today the business is part of the One-Stop brand.

What was the good news Bea had received? Perhaps it was the news that Florence had returned home to live.

NEWCASTLE ON TYNE. HIGH LEVEL & SWING BRIDGES.   Copyright.

POST CARD.

LONDON.S.W.

FOR INLAND POSTAGE. THIS SPACE, AS
WELL AS THE BACK, MAY NOW BE
USED FOR COMMUNICATION.
FOR FOREIGN POSTAGE THE BACK ONLY.
(Post Office Regulation).

THE ADDRESS ONLY TO BE
WRITTEN HERE

Please thank
mum for Paper
C.W

Miss E. Berwick
The Cottage
14. Broadwater Down
Tunbridge Wells

087046

225

087046
1905
Miss E Berwick
The Cottage
14 Broadwater Down
Tunbridge Wells
Please thank Mum for paper
CW

Edith (b.1890) is listed as a housemaid in 1911, at 8 Calverley Terrace, Tunbridge Wells. Her employer was a widow, Katherine Dixon (b.1840), and her daughter Eliza Dixon (b.1866) also lived at the address.

In 1901, Edith lived at home in The Cottage with her parents, Alfred (b.1850) and Martha née Down (b.1854), and her sister Kate (b.1884). Alfred was a gardener and Kate was a housemaid.

Edith married Frederick Birchby (b.1885) in 1926. By 1939 she was a widow, living with her mother. Her employment was listed as domestic duties and gate-keeper in Uckfield.

Kate married William Balkham (b.1874) in 1934 and in 1939 she was a widow, working as a between maid.

Who is the card from? I knew from the 1911 census that Alfred and Martha had four children and that by 1911 two had died. Alice (b.1885) had died in 1887. George (b.1891) had died in the year of his birth. That only left Kate. Was she known as Cathy? No, I believe the card was from someone else – CW is still to be found.

Lynmouth, Watersmeet

POST CARD

Communication

We spent last week at
Minehead, are now at
Lynmouth, + are shortly moving
on, I expect to Barnstable
+ Bideford. The weather is
being very kind to us on the
whole, as we have not been
kept in by rain at all, but it
is very sunless + the wind
very cold. Hope you are
keeping well. Love - W.B.

Address

Mrs. Sherriff
10 Mount Pleasant
Cheshunt
Herts.

088027

227

088027

13 September 1912
Mrs Sherriff
10 Mount Pleasant
Cheshurst, Herts.

We spent last week at Minehead, are now at Lynmouth, and are shortly moving on, I expect to Barnstable and Bideford. The weather is being very kind to us on the whole, as we have not been kept in by rain at all, but it is very xxxx and the wind very cold. Hope you are keeping well. Love WB.

In 1911, Emily Sherriff née Briden (b.1875) lived with husband, William (b.1863), a nurseryman engineer. It was clear in the 1911 census that the couple had married in 1897, and where they had been born – Emily in Stevenage, Hertfordshire and William in Dalkeith, Scotland. They had no children at this time.

In 1901, they lived in Broad Street, Bath. However, at this time William's occupation is veterinary surgeon. Is it the correct couple? Their ages matched, and their places of birth. I created their tree but wasn't convinced – so I returned to 1911 and began again, with the same result. I looked at some of the other trees created. They too had the same results as I'd had. There is absolutely no reason why a vet cannot become a nurseryman – but is it correct?

I decided to focus on the wife's tree and began from scratch. Soon, despite trying to ignore the marriage to a vet, I was back with that marriage – him as a vet, her father Thomas Briden (b.1845) as a draper – which fitted the census returns. I continued to follow Emily and her siblings. Franklin (b.1873) was a grocer in 1901. Hilda (b.1878) and Ruby (b.1882) are both listed as assistant drapers in 1901.

Back to William. I decided to review all of the other trees available. I found one that listed some half-siblings. Could that be the answer? No. It was a muddled tree, full of obvious errors including parents born after their children. Was there a simple answer to this problem? Could William have changed careers? In 1891, he was living as a boarder with a vet – and his occupation is listed as a vet. The location? Stevenage. Is this where Emily and William met?

Because I had the information from the 1911 census, I decided to have one final search for a marriage between a William Sherriff and a spouse with the first name Emily. I opened it up by a year either side of 1897. I still found only one.

Who was William Sherriff? He had at least four siblings – Christian (b.1852), Euphemia (b.1852), Isabella (b.1854) and James (b.1858). His parents were William (b.1821) and Christian née Purves (b.1826).

Town Hall. Leeds.

POST CARD GREAT BRITAIN & IRELAND
THE ADDRESS ONLY TO BE WRITTEN ON THIS SIDE.

HALF PENNY

Mr. Granville Chapman
Baltimore House
Hainton St.
Grimsby.

089044

089044
Saturday Jan 24 1908
Mrs Granville Chapman
Baltimore House
Hawton St
Grimsby
This is a lovely place inside.
Thanks dears, shall be delighted to come & have tea with you tomorrow.
I'm afraid G will be asking if I have brought my luggage. Have been in the town shopping
all the morning. Mother has bought me three lovely blouses. Am I not lucky?
I was sorry about yesterday afternoon. I had been out all the morning shopping & then we
had a friend for tea. So I couldn't manage it.
The multitudes are racing by to the match. I am wondering if your dear little [?] is in the
crowds. Good-bye till tomorrow. Heaps of love to you all from [?]. Am coming early
tomorrow

The sender of this card clearly wanted to make the most her postage charge – it's such a detailed message. I was unable to trace the recipient in 1911. However, Amy Chapman née Treliving (b.1876) was living at the address in 1901, with her husband Charles Leopold *Granville* Chapman (b.1876) and their son, Lionel Valentine Granville Chapman. Lionel was born on 14 February 1901.

In 1901, Granville is recorded as a physician surgeon. He would later become a consulting surgeon and appears in several directories in Grimsby and London as a doctor. When Amy and Granville married in 1899, both their fathers were listed as merchants. In 1881, Granville's father, Charles (b.1848), was listed as a cattle oil manufacturer. In 1911, Granville's brother, Harold (b.1879), was listed as a cattle medicine manufacturer. By 1939 he was a director of a company that manufactured veterinary medicine.

When I began creating Amy Treliving's tree I was concerned about the number of siblings I had found – 11 including Amy. By 1911, her father Alfred (b.1845) had died, so the 1911 census wouldn't necessarily tell me how many children her mother, Mary née Beasant (b.1842), had had. Fortunately for me she'd completed her return incorrectly and declared she had 14 children and four had died. At least one of the 11 I had found had died by 1911 – so I know there are gaps in Amy's branch.

Alfred Treliving was an ironmonger, born in Plymouth and trading in London. In 1901, he is listed as an employer. A notice in the *London Gazette* mentions that Alfred was in partnership with George Smith, trading at two addresses: 100–101 Minories, London and in Balham. The partnership was dissolved in 1891. The Minories, I discovered, is not far from the Tower of London. Unfortunately the area has been redeveloped.

Lionel joined the Royal Navy and I found him serving in the First World

War with the rank of lieutenant-commander. At the beginning of the Second World War he was employed as a hospital administrator.

Who sent the postcard? I'm unsure. I did consider one of Amy's sisters – but the card was posted in Grimsby and I could only trace the sisters in the London area. What about Granville's sisters? I began with his mother. Margaret née Bennington (b.1849) appears in the 1911 census as a widow living with her daughter, Lily (b.1884), and son-in-law, Robert Moffatt (b.1859). Margaret's entry was also incorrect – it declared she had had 10 children and three had died. I hadn't found all of those 10 children – and those that I had didn't match with the card.

With a total of 20 siblings between them, I was unable to trace who Granville and Amy's visitor was – and she may not even have been a relative.

Somerset & Dorset joint Ry. 4 Coupled bogie express.

Chem. Lab.
114 Clements Rd
East Ham. E.

POST CARD

For INLAND Postage this Space, as well as the
Back, may now be used for Communication,
For FOREIGN Postage the Back only. 1/4/10
(Post Office Regulation.)

The address only to be written

Dear A.   Regret inability
to obtain white lead by
Saturday as I shall not
be going straight home from
business on Fri. & Sat. (same
to-day) & one cannot stow away
4 tons of paint in a waist-coat pocket.
Please notify if too-late, if not come
for it one evening after Monday next.
Can I send you any tickets (6d or 1/-)
for Emmanuel Gym. Display April 23
Hope you will come

H. G. Foster, Esq.
12 Kenilworth Gardens
Seven Kings
Essex.

LONDON
S.E.

08 6045

090003

090003
April 1910
HG Foster Esq
12 Kenilworth Gardens
Seven Kings
Essex
Dear H.
Regret inability to obtain white lead by Saturday as I shall not be going straight home from business on Friday and Saturday (same to-day) and one cannot stow away 1 ton of paint in a waistcoat pocket. Please notify if too late, if not come for it one evening after Monday next. Can I send you any tickets 6D 1/- for Emmanuel Gym display April 23? Hope you will come.
Reg.
ink = alkaline blue and patent blue
Chem. Lab.
114 Clements Road
East Ham

Having the sender's address on the card certainly adds to the message – sent from a chemical lab in East Ham. Or was it?

The card was sent to Harold Foster in Seven Kings, Essex. Harold (b.1889) was the son of a schoolteacher, Josiah Foster (b.1863), and Clara née Eames (b.1861). In 1910, when the card was sent, Harold was an assistant working in Customs and Excise. He married Ivy née Wenman (b.1896) in 1919. In 1939 Harold was a civil servant, still with Customs and Excise.

Ivy's father was an engineer with the Post Office. In 1911, a sister, Edith (b.1891), worked as a female sorter with the Post Office. In 1912, Ivy is listed in postal services records as a telephone operator. Another sister, Dorothy (b.1900), became a bookkeeper.

The card, from the lab in East Ham, was sent by Reginald Phillips (b.1889). The address on the card is actually his home address – in 1911, he lived with his parents. Alfred (b.1861) and Selina (b.1861) Phillips had three children. Alfred was a commercial clerk for a tar distiller.

Reg was an assistant chemist in the colour trade. His sister, Dorothy (b.1891), was a shorthand typist. Leonard (b.1896) served in the First World War. His service records confirm his address as being at 114 Clements Road.

In 1939, Reg was living with his wife Ruby and his occupation was chemical practitioner (pigment dyestuffs).

Clearly paint and colours were important to Reg – he had added the ink details to the card: *alkaline blue and patent blue*. That shade is still vibrant on the card today – much brighter than the more common dark ink that was often used.

Emmanuel Church in Forest Gate had a hall and it is likely that this was where the gym display was being held. The hall has a history of fitness and body-building. In more recent years, 'Wag' Bennett used it as a bodybuilding gym. Wag's most famous protégé was Arnold Schwarzenegger (b.1947) who stayed with the Bennett family for several months. There are a number of online articles about Wag and Arnie's association, including the E7-NowAndThen.org site where you will find some fascinating images of the hall – and Arnie.

POST CARD.

This Space may be used for Correspondence.
For INLAND (not Foreign) POSTAGE.

FOR ADDRESS ONLY.

10/11/11

Wishing you many happy
Returns of the day.
Hope all are well. Love
to us all. B.M.

Miss L. Wakely
Morden Mills
Wareham.

091086

091086
10 November 1911
Miss L Wakely
Morden Mills
Wareham
Wishing you many Happy Returns of the day.
Hope all are well.
Love from us all.
BM

Lily Wakely (b.1887) was one of seven children. In 1911, she lived with her parents, Henry (b.1855) and Martha née Hansford (b.1854), widowed sister Olive née Young (b.1880), and Olive's son, Donald (b.1908).

As soon as I began creating the family's tree I discovered who the card had most likely been sent by. However, I initially focused on the parents.

Henry Wakely was born in Beaminster, Dorset. His father was a farmer. Henry and Martha married in 1874 and in 1881 they lived in the Wareham area where Henry farmed 216 acres. By 1901, the family had returned to Beaminster. In 1911, when the postcard was sent, Henry was listed as a miller and farmer – at Morden Mills which is near Wareham.

Martha was born near Portesham, Dorset and she lived with her parents, William (b.1817) and Ann Hansford (b.1814), on a dairy farm.

Their first child, Bessie, was born in 1875 in Beaminster. In 1901, she worked as an assistant in a dairy. She married John Matthews (b.1879), a dairy manager, and the couple lived in Piddletrenthide – which suggests the birthday card was sent by Bessie.

Emily was born in 1877 and in 1911 she lived with a widowed aunt – Ellen Cox (b.1851) in Sherborne, Dorset. Emily married Clifford Barrett (b.1870), a builder, and they lived in Beaminster.

Edith (b.1880) married James Kennard (b.1870), a grocer from Rugby, Warwickshire, and the couple also lived in Beaminster.

Florence (b.1883) married Thomas Marsh (b.1880) and the couple lived in Organford – a few miles away from Morden. Thomas was a farmer and miller.

Eva (b.1886) married William Burr (b.1854), a famer in Morden.

Lily (b.1887) married Leonard Parsons (b.1895), a builder from Swanage. By a strange twist of fate, the couple lived in a house opposite to the one my parents lived in for a number of years. Leonard's family are well known in Swanage as builders and they built many of the houses in that part of the town.

Finally to Olive. She had married Alfred Young (b.1877) and he died in 1910. Alfred was a butcher and at the time of their marriage, lived in Sussex – where Alfred was born.

After Alfred's death, Olive married Walter Dredge (b.1880), a farmer from Somerset. Walter was a widower and he already had a child, Ivy (b.1905). His first wife was Ethel née Wakely (b.1877) – a cousin of Olive's.

Walter and Ethel emigrated to America and Ivy was born in Nebraska.

Olive sailed to America with Donald in 1912 – a few months after she had appeared in the 1911 census return with her parents in Morden.

Walter and Olive had at least two daughters together and the family remained in America.

This particular postcard was not the most interesting on first appearance – a black and white photograph of a church, a short message, and even the stamp had been removed. However, possibly because of my own links to the areas mentioned, I found it fascinating. Olive in particular seemed to share an inspirational tale, perhaps one of hardship and sadness. I can never know the story behind the facts – but I do hope she and Walter were happy. I don't believe they had an easy life – living on a farm in Nebraska.

Just as I was researching this story, Morden Mills appeared in the local press. It had been sold at auction for £360,000. Part of the large Drax Estate, it formed 6.52 acres of pasture land. The derelict buildings will be transformed, I'm sure, into a magnificent dwelling – and the story of those who call it home will continue.

Den and Pier, Teignmouth

Dear Mr McKee
received your Cards
glad to hear you
got back safe Love
to miss Kirste and
except the same
your Self from
us all we are all
well hope to see
you soon from J K

Mr J McKee
No 58 Rutland
St Stepney
London
E

092087

092087
30 April 1911
Mr J McKee
58 Rutland Street
Stepney
London
Dear Mr McKee
Received your cards something to here you got back and love to miss Charlotte and something be something so is all we are all well hope to see you soon from J Le.

In all honesty this card shouldn't be included in this book. My research is inconclusive and raises more questions than it answers.

I found James McKee at the address as a boarder in 1911. At that time he was a carpenter and his age was given as 31. In 1901, he was a boarder at the same address with an age of 24. Because I had no family details and an inconclusive year of birth, I decided to move on to his landlady, Elizabeth Christer. Her details were also confusing. In 1911, she was 49, but 10 years earlier the census has her at the same address with the same boarder and being 43 years old.

In 1891, I found her at 74 Rutland Street with her mother, also named Elizabeth. The census shows her age as 39, although Ancestry had translated that to a birth year of 1852.

In 1881, her mother was at that address with her brother. At this time the mother is shown as being born in Germany. Her age is 10 years out and the brother's is three years out.

In 1871, Elizabeth and her brother are at 74 Rutland Street and her age is given as 25. The census notes that the mother is the head of the household but is absent. That results in Henry being listed as his sister's son. Also at the address was William Fugeman and he is listed as being the son of the head of the household. I decided to create a tree for William but couldn't find anything definite.

Of course, the mother Elizabeth, daughter Elizabeth and Henry might all be correctly dated – perhaps they are different people with the same names living at the same addresses as the others. Unlikely?

I have no explanation as to why the ages vary. It's not unusual to find some discrepancies but this story really was a comedy of errors. Because the family stayed in the same area and at the same addresses for long periods, I'm as certain as I can be that I've followed the family correctly. Purchasing their respective birth certificates would, of course, help solve the problem. However, I decided that it would be as interesting to show the questions raised. Genealogy can be so frustrating!

A. Benzaquen, Tanger.

2.

29.2.12.
Thanks for letter received before we started.
The smells here are de-lightful as it needs no police to keep the crowd moving.
I have seen Swallows & other Summer migrants. The Gib. Rock was wonderful. BHB.

MOROCCO AGENCIES 10 CENTIMOS

TANGIER 3 PM 29 FE 12

C. Holme-Barnett Esq.
"Coonoor"
Fairfield Park Rd.
Leckhampton.
Cheltenham.
England.

093097

Viertel der Eingeborenen, Mazagan.
(Native Quarter).

POSTKARTE — CARTE-POST
Weltpostverein-Union Postale Universell

I should like you to see one of these Moorish cities, they are filthy dirty but the people at so interesting all shouting & jostling. the water carrier with his goat Skin full of water interests me - there are Riff Moors Arabs - Sahara men &c we see a caravan of camels that going into the town —

Thos H. Barnett
Sidcot School
Winscombe
Somerset
England -

093097

241

093097

B.P.148-Madeira. Camara de Lobos.   Registado.

093097
1910
Sidcot School
Winscombe, Somerset
England
I should like you to see one of these Moorish cities they are filthy dirty but the people are so interesting all shouting and jostling – the water carrier with his goat-skin full of water interests me.
There are Riff Moor Arabs – Sahara maybe.
We see a caravan of camels just going into the town.

26 February 1910
Sidcot School
Winscombe, Somerset
England
You would have laughed at seeing us on camel back today.
Father took a super shot.
Uncle T

29 February 1912
C Holme-Barnett Esq
"Coonor"
Fairfield Park Road
Leckhampton, Cheltenham
England
Thanks for letter received before we started.
The smells here are delightful as it needs no police so as to keep the crowd moving.
I have seen swallows and other summer migrants.
The Gib. Rock was wonderful.
BB

13 March 1912
C Holme-Barnett Esq
"Coonor"
Fairfield Park Road
Leckhampton
Cheltenham, England
Just been up the funicular rly here –
Same as Ken went up.
Fancy Dress Ball last night – I went as a baby and another fellow as my nurse.
No cigars here at all!
Can't see any anywhere.

244

I'm so pleased I broke my own rule and bought more than one postcard for the same family story. The family that sent the postcards were clearly lovers of travel and the cards were sent from two trips – in 1910 and 1912. Two postcards were sent to a son at his school and the others to another family member at his home.

John Barnett (b.1859) and Sarah née Saul (b.1861) had five children, and by 1911 one child had died. Sarah's father, Dan Saul (b.1830), is shown in Society of Friends and census records as being a manufacturer. Her mother was Sophia née Holme (b.1835) – which nicely explains the family's middle name – sometimes found as being hyphenated with the surname.

John Barnett's brother, Charles (b.1861), was a cashier for a jeweller. In 1911, his profession also showed that he was a director of a jewellery company.

What happened to John and Sarah's children? Charles (b.1887) became a dentist. He appears in passenger lists in 1934, aboard *Highland Monarch* and *Highland Princess* sailing from Argentina, Shanghai and Spain. Wilfrid (b.1889) died in infancy. Brian (b.1893) became a bank clerk and Thomas (b.1898) died during the First World War. Thomas sent the postcard that mentions camels.

Kenneth (b.1891) served in the First World War. He later emigrated to South Africa and managed a fruit farm. His journeys can be followed in various passenger lists, sailing to and from South Africa: 1931 *Arundel Castle*, 1914 and 1924 *Ceramic*, 1937 *Themistocles*.

Unsurprisingly, given the postcards, I also found the parents in various passenger lists including sailing to South Africa in 1925 aboard *Ascanius*.

I had managed to create the family's tree without any difficulty. However, I wasn't sure who the children actually were in regards to the postcards. I decided to contact the school. Christine Gladwin, Sidcot School Archivist, responded to my query and provided me with the following additional information. Christine was able to share a considerable amount from the Old Scholars' Register. In fact she knew Anthony Holme Barnett (b.1927) quite well. Anthony was at the school during the Second World War and he received the most recent postcard that isn't included here but you can view via the link that's found in the final section of this book. Here's what Christine told me:

He used to come to reunions at school and he contributed a lot to books I wrote about the history of the school in the first half of the 20th century. He was very interested in how things worked and could remember arcane facts about such things as the laundry machinery!

She also told me that all four of John and Lilian's children attended the school.

Brian Holme Barnett was at the school from 1904–1910. He was Junior and Senior sports champion. In 1911, he entered the National Provincial Bank and then joined the Friends Ambulance Unit Agricultural Section during the First World War. In 1919 he started his own market garden and from 1928 to 1947 he was Warden of Conference House in Welwyn.

Charles Holme Barnett attended the school from 1899–1904.

Kenneth Holme Barnett attended the school from 1902–1907. In 1908 he went to South Africa, becoming manager of one of the large Cecil Rhodes fruit farms. He joined the RFA during the First World War and was wounded in France and taken prisoner. He developed his own fruit farm and died in South Africa.

Thomas Holme Barnett attended the school from 1909–1914. On leaving the school he offered himself for the Friends Ambulance Service and trained at Oxhey Grange Camp. As he was underage he was unable to go to France immediately, but having been accepted by the Unit he was looking forward to active service. However, he became ill in August 1915 and died of typhoid a few weeks later. Tom had been an excellent athlete and 'all a happy English schoolboy should be, honest, keen, enthusiastic, lovable – clean and alert in body and mind'. (Review of the Terms 1915).

The information provided by Christine adds so much to this particular story. I'm pleased that the details I had researched were correct (where that information was repeated by Christine I have not included it again), but it was wonderful to hear about the family's involvement with the school and have that special connection.

TINTERNS ABBY

POST CARD

BRADFORD
4. 15 PM
MAR 29 11

THE ADDRESS ONLY TO BE
WRITTEN HERE.

HALF PENNY

Dear Jack,
Ith
auntie Blanche for
de kind invitation,
and I am looking
forward to coming
on Saturday, I will
bring my albums,
and some flower seeds for
you. Raymond

Master J Elliot

16 Sherwood Grove

Nab Wood

N^s Bfd.

094078

247

094078
29 March 1911
Master J Elliot
16 Sherwood Grove, Nab Wood
Nr Bradford
Dear Jock
Thank auntie Blanche for the kind invitation, and I am looking forward to coming ton
Saturday, I will bring my albums, and some flower series for you.
Raymond

There's always something very touching about postcards sent to and from young children and this one is no exception. The 1911 census has George Tredwell Elliott (b.1902) living at the address with his widowed mother Blanche Elliott née Speight (b.1866).

Although Tredwell sounded an unusual name, so many children were given the surnames of their grandparents and other relatives that I didn't question it – at that time. However, his birth records confirmed that George's middle name was actually Frederick and had been transcribed incorrectly – and that proved interesting as I developed his family's tree.

Blanche married Frederick Elliott (b.1858) in 1902 and he died in 1911 – just days before the census had been taken. Blanche was the daughter of Frederick (b.1831) and Mary Speight (b.1835). Frederick's occupation is listed as a stuff (textile) merchant manager – many of their neighbours worked in this industry.

Frederick was the son of George (b.1829) and Mary née Farrar (b.1829). George was also involved in the stuff industry and in 1861, was a manager. Ten years later and he was a buyer. By 1891, he and Mary had relocated and I found them living in Westbourne, Hampshire – now Dorset. Two daughters – Isabel (b.1866) and Grace (b.1870) – had also moved to the area. The family moved again, this time to Wimborne, Dorset.

Frederick was also involved in the textile industry. His probate records confirm he was a manufacturer. In earlier records, I found him as worsted manufacturer.

Who was Raymond? Although he mentions 'auntie' Blanche, it's never certain that the person will actually be a relative. I looked at both Frederick and Blanche's siblings and created their trees. Blanche's sister, Mary (b.1858), married Edmund Heaton (b.1858) in 1879 and the youngest child I traced was Raymond (b.1898).

Raymond appears in several online trees and lived into his seventies. George – Jock – was harder to trace. He appeared in several trees as George *Tredwell* Elliott – which rang alarm bells. If those researchers hadn't resolved that incorrect name I would have to reject anything else they shared. However, I did find that George also lived into his seventies.

NATIVE WOMAN.

Carte postale Universelle.

LONDON

Port Said
May 4th 1912

Dear Flori.
We arrived here last
night. Leave tomorrow for
Malta. R.M.S. Spartak for
here going to take in to
relive the "Minshiri" love
to "xxxx" xxx xxx
to "xxxx". xxxx xxxx

Master C. Oates.
8 Harveys Bldgs
Dorchester
Dorset
England

095085

249

095085
Port Said
7 May 1912
Master C Oates
8 Harveys Bldgs
Dorchester
Dorset
England
Dear Char.
We arrived here last night, leave tomorrow for Malta. The HMS Spartiate is here going to China to relieve the Minotaur.
Love to all
Will.

I found Will's family in 1911 living in Dorchester. Charles (b.1845) and Jane née Edmonds (b.1855) had nine children and by the time of the census two had died. Living at the address were Edward *George* (b.1884), Ethel (b.1895) and Herbert *Charles* (b.1898). I would later discover Rosa (b.1879), Emma (b.1881) and Dora (b.1888) – making seven of the nine.

Charles senior was the son of George (b.1798) and Hannah Oates (b.1794) and was born in Wiltshire. In 1871, he was a servant working in the Ward Room for the Royal Navy in Sheerness. Ten years later and he was married and living with Jane in Pylle, Somerset and worked as a coachman. By 1891, the family had moved to Dorchester where he worked as a groom. Later, he would become a grocer's porter and a gardener.

Jane née Edmonds was born in Wareham, Dorset. In the earlier census returns I found her living with an uncle and then her grandparents – John and Ann Edmonds – in Langton Matravers, an area known for stone quarrying. John was a stonemason.

Although I only discovered seven of the children, I was able to follow them through several detailed trails.

Rosa was born in Basingstoke, Hampshire. In 1901, she worked as a servant for a retired bank manager in Swanage, Dorset. In 1911, she had relocated to London and worked in Kensington for a widow. The address is a short walk from Harrods.

Emma, George and Dora were born in Pylle. In 1901, Emma was working as a servant in Torquay, Devon. Ten years later she was a cook in Surrey working for a barrister and his family. George worked as a baker in Somerset, living in the bake house. He joined the family in Dorchester where he continued to work as a baker. Dora worked as a servant in Bournemouth. She later married an insurance agent from the town.

Ethel was born in Dorchester and was a dressmaker's apprentice. She later married a driver.

Charles, to whom the postcard was addressed, was the youngest child that I was able to trace and he was born in Dorchester. He became a civil servant and worked for the county courts.

In 1939, Rosa, Emma and William lived together in Wandsworth. From his Royal Navy records I discovered more than just the facts about William's career. I found, for example, that he had several tattoos – one being that of a Japanese woman. At the time the card was sent, William was aboard HMS *Hawke*. He remained with the navy throughout the First World War. He died in 1942 and in his naval records it states that at the time of his death he was serving on HMS *Wellesley*. He died in the Royal Naval hospital in Seaforth, Liverpool. His naval trade was baker.

096126
2 February 1907
Miss May Harrison
45 Bygrave Lane
Baldock
Herts.
Dear M
A line hoping all are well.
I have just taken a fancy to this card hoping you will keep them all.
I will try and get a few more for you.
Lottie sends her best love to you all with my best love from your loving brother.
EGH

I found May in 1911 – Gertrude May Harrison (b.1900) – living with her family. Edward (b.1859) and Mary née Bardle (b.1858) had nine children, and by the time of the census one had died. Edward was a railway porter.

The children living at home in 1911 were Jessie (b.1892), Amy (b.1893) and Bertha (b.1896). Jessie was listed as a teacher, Amy a bookkeeper and Bertha a domestic nurse. Another daughter, Mabel (b.1887), was listed in 1911 as working as a cook for a farmer in Norfolk. I traced three brothers – Ernest (b.1884), Edwin George Harrison – EGH (b.1885), and William (b.1889). William married Lily née Hyde in 1912 and their son, Graham Harrison (b.1912), would serve in the RAF as a pilot. In 1944, as Flight Lieutenant Harrison, he was shot down and killed in the Bay of Biscay. He has a grave in Bilbao, Spain.

The postcard was sent to May by her brother Edwin. In 1911, he lived in Portsmouth with his wife, Charlotte née Cauvin (b.1887), and their daughter, Mabel (b.1910). His occupation is listed as 2nd ship's cook Royal Navy. Also at the address was Lewis Cauvin (b.1844), a naval pensioner.

Edwin served on HMS *Hampshire* and although the ship was present at the Battle of Jutland, some websites state the ship remained in a support role. On 5 June, after the battle, *Hampshire* sailed for north Russia on a diplomatic mission. The ship is believed to have struck a minefield and an explosion caused catastrophic damage to the ship. It took barely 15 minutes for the ship to sink. Only 12 members of the 735 crew and 14 passengers survived. Edwin was one of those who perished – alongside the Secretary of State for War, Field Marshal Lord Kitchener (b.1850).

Kitchener's body was never recovered and there is a memorial to him at Marwick Head in Orkney – near to where the ship sank.

The Orkney Heritage Society curates a website and they have an image of Jessie Cumloquoy. She was the postmistress at Birsay who had responded to the sight of a ship in distress and was able to send a telegram on behalf of the military lookout personnel within minutes – before the ship sank.

Edwin's grave is in Lyness Royal Naval Cemetery, on Hoy in Orkney. There are many official websites that show images of the memorials, but I came across a blog that lists all the names with an image of their respective headstone. The blog is anonymous and seems to have been created just for that purpose – to provide an image and relevant details. The blog has no followers and there are no owner details. Edwin is listed as chief cook. I posted a 'thank you' comment that would be published after approval. It never was.

I found several possible marriages for May – but was unable to confirm precisely which – if any – might be hers. The postcard is one of the most creased and damaged in this collection. Yet, to May and to this book, it's priceless.

097032

097032
12 August 1906
Mrs Jones
28 Burdett Street
St Michaels
Liverpool
Dear Mother and All
The weather here is still very unsettled still.
We hope to leave Grimsby tomorrow about 2.30pm hope to be home about 7pm.
Love from both.
Will

In 1911, Emily Jones née Crease (b.1851) lived with ship joiner husband Samuel (b.1857) and son Ernest (b.1888), a messenger. The couple had eight children and by the time of the 1911 census two had died.

William (b.1880) – Will – is listed in 1911, as a shipping clerk. He married Annie née Wilkinson (b.1880) in 1910 and the couple lived near his parents.

Although I'm certain that Will sent the card (the handwriting matches his entry in the 1911 census), I wonder who 'both' refers to. Will and Annie didn't marry until four years later and at that time Will was a bachelor.

My initial research didn't reveal much beyond the usual births, marriages and deaths for the family. However, once I began to look at Emily in more detail I realised that the story of her life was well worth recording.

Emily was born in Somerset and in 1861, at the age of 10, she was working for a laundress and baker in Bath. Ten years later and she was still in Bath, working for another family as a cook. Her father, James Crease (b.1811), was an agricultural labourer. Knowing that a child had left home and was working is not new knowledge – however, Emily must have been at least 10 when she began work. Perhaps the home and life she shared with her employers was better than the one her parents were able to provide.

When she married in 1877, she recorded no employment but was living in the Liverpool area. Samuel and Emma appear in the 1881 census living with Samuel's parents – Samuel (b.1828) and Hannah née Davidson (b.1823). Hannah was a midwife. By 1881, the couple had their own home in Mill Street, the same street as Samuel's family. The house in Burdett Street (the address on the card) is still there – even the tiles that lead to the front door are in situ. A peek inside a neighbouring property via an estate agent's website reveals the original feature of fireplaces. The rooms are small – especially when considering the size of Emily's family.

Although Emily had signed the marriage register, her signature didn't flow with the same ease the others appear to have. Perhaps she had learnt to sign her name by copying it. A generation later and it's so very different. Their eldest daughter, Hannah (b.1878), became a teacher and we know Will, who sent the card, was a clerk. There's no doubt Emily had a hard life. Even when married, it wouldn't have been much easier than when she was a child. However, what she and her husband did do was provide a home for their children and a life where they could be educated.

The Elementary Education Act 1870 established schools for children aged from five to 10. Ten years later, another act made it compulsory for children to be educated. It was 11 years later, in 1891, before education became free. Emily (b.1851) was born too early to benefit from those immense changes.

Although it was made illegal in 1843 to employ children under the age of nine, Emily and her childhood contemporaries could work a 48-hour week.

As I approach the end of these stories, with only one left, I can't help feeling that Emily's story speaks as much about our history and social change as those connected with the stories of national and international events: child worker, wife and mother. That she, a young girl who left home to work and was poorly educated, raised a family that included someone who would teach the children of the next generation, tells me more about the spirit of the people I've researched than perhaps anything else can.

116. Bruxelles Palais du Roi - Brussel Kouing's Paleis
Brussels King's Hall

Dear Mam and Dad,

We are still having
a good. We arrived
from LUXEMBURG this
afternoon. Yesterday we
went to the 'RADIO
LUXEMBURG relay station

The flags are still
out here at Brussels,
and it's a public holiday.
with love John

BELGIQUE
AGRICULTURE
2.50
FR BELGIE

MR & MRS. A. BAGGOTT

LINGARD

BRIARS ROAD

OLDBURY

BIRMINGHAM
ENGLAND.

098124

098124
Mr & Mrs A Baggott
Lingard
Brades Road
Oldbury, Birmingham
Dear Mam and Dad
We are still having a good [time]. We arrived from Luxemburg this afternoon. Yesterday we went to the Radio Luxemburg relay station.
The flags are still out here at Brussels and it's a public holiday.
With love.
John

This collection of stories finishes with a postcard sent in the 1950s to an address in Oldbury, Birmingham. The recipients are my grandparents and the card was sent by my father. I'm not sure exactly when the card was sent. It could have been when he was at agricultural college, or maybe it was when Dad worked on a dairy farm in Inkberrow, Worcestershire. I do know who organised the trip. Aunt Sarah (b.1893) – my grandmother Beatrice's sister – was going on a coach trip with a friend and invited Dad to join them. Sarah had spent most of her life as a widow – her husband, Frederick Willshaw (b.1887), died shortly before the birth of their daughter Beatrice – always known as Mary – in 1921.

In with the postcard, Dad had kept two small pieces of ephemera – brochures of two hotels. Without the link to the postcard, their relevance would be lost. Not only do I know where Dad visited, I also know the hotels in which they stayed – Hotel Francia in Paris and Hotel Des Ardennes in Belgium – which was, apparently, *confort modern* and had a *jardin*.

Had this been a card I was researching from scratch, I know I would have felt a frisson of excitement as I discovered that his maternal grandmother's maiden name was also the name of the house – *Lingard*. I would also have experienced frustration when I eventually realised that despite signing the card John, the sender's registered name was Arthur (b.1933) – that's so typical of a lot of postcards and is a priceless insight into how the senders and recipients were known to their friends and family.

Several cousins began completing the Baggott branch of my tree long before I became interested in genealogy. Those early printouts were peppered with errors. Showing my father as John was always an indication of how much had been researched – very often the names were added from personal knowledge and that's a lesson to us all. Even what you know can be wrong.

My paternal grandfather, Arthur Baggott (b.1901), had three siblings, but by 1911, two had died – Rosina (b.1899) at a few months and William (b.1897) who was only eight when he drowned. His father, Simon (b.1873), worked for the council gas works. A generation later and so would his son, my grandfather. Simon and my great-grandmother, Rosina née Leonard (b.1874), appear on the front cover of this book.

My paternal grandmother, Beatrice née Osborne (b.1901), was born in Smethwick. Her father, Joseph (b.1863), was a puddler in an ironworks. In 1891, Joseph and Sarah née Lingard (b.1864) lived next door to Sarah's parents.

Calling the family's home Lingard wasn't necessarily the only reason my grandparents wanted to remember my great-grandmother's maiden name. Sarah's father was Thomas Lingard (b.1843) and one of his siblings was Daniel Lingard (b.1847). Although he was originally a grocer, Daniel became a pottery manufacturer in Stoke-on-Trent and he is the Lingard in Lingard Webster, a factory that produced tea ware.

In 1912, just before Daniel died, Clarice Cliff (b.1899) began an apprenticeship with the factory as an enameller and according to more than one website was paid one shilling a week. Daniel was my great-great-great-uncle and a distant relative. Despite that, my family are proud to own several pieces of pottery produced by his factory. More personally, he appears in the probate records for Thomas Lingard (b.1816). Thomas was Daniel's father and my great-great-great-grandfather.

My grandparents were Methodists and my grandfather was a chapel organist. A family story tells of how my grandmother, Beatrice, would be sent with her sister to stay with an aunt and uncle that ran a pub. This seemed an unlikely piece of family folklore. However, Joseph Osborne's brother, Richard (b.1871), married Sarah Lingard's sister, Hannah (b.1872), and the couple ran the Five Ways beer house in Silverdale, Staffordshire. Their customers would have been coalminers and foundry workers. Hannah continued to run the business after Richard's death.

My father served in the RAF for his National Service and was stationed at Worth Matravers, near Swanage in Dorset. He met my mother, Gillian née Tatchell (b.1941), and they married in 1958 in St Mary's church (see the postcard on page 104). Although Mum is known as Gill, her registered name is Jillian – the family trait of confusing first names is found in both branches of my tree.

Mum's family tree has always been a challenge. Her father, Albert Tatchell (b.1900), was born in Swanage and the Tatchell family has been researched and recorded by many cousins. The Tatchells came to the Swanage area centuries ago from Somerset. There are some records that indicate the name travelled from France with the Huguenots. There's little doubt that they moved from an area of Somerset known for quarrying because of the opportunities in the Purbeck stone quarries that surround Swanage.

My maternal grandmother, Violet née Abbott (b.1910), was born in London. Her family tree has tested me – often I've taken a break and returned to it only to be rewarded with more frustration. It was quite a moment when I realised that my grandmother's mother, Ellen née Harris (b.1876), had recorded the births of two of her children incorrectly – providing her own mother's maiden name instead of her own. There was a family story about an Abbott marrying a Monk. That proved to be untrue – a Monk married a Harris and their daughter married the Abbott.

I never knew my maternal grandfather. Albert Tatchell was killed in 1953. He was sailing from Stranraer to Larne on the MV *Princess Victoria*. More than 130 people lost their lives – a disaster caused by bad weather, bad decisions and bad equipment. The ship's radio officer, David Broadfoot (b.1899), was posthumously awarded the George Cross for staying at his post. The captains of other vessels were also commended for their attempts to rescue survivors. There were only 44 survivors – none of them members of the crew. At a time when we wrote letters rather than emails, I researched the tragedy. I wanted to know more about what had killed my grandfather and forced my mother to grow up without her father. Today, decades after that research, I know it's helped me connect with the tragedies I've discovered in this book and treat them with compassion.

Albert served in the First and Second World Wars – he enlisted with the newly formed Royal Air Force on 13 April 1918 – his 18th birthday. You can see Albert with his brother, Kenneth (b.1919), who was killed during the Second World War, on the back of this book's cover.

Dad's postcard is a fitting way to conclude this book. After all, it was my parents buying Gilbert Freeman's cards that started me on this journey. Some of the stories associated with the postcards are brief – little more than the black and white facts. However, they all come alive because of those pieces of card. In some ways they're as important as a photograph, offering an insight into their daily lives.

Through the postcards I've learned about the relationships, the living conditions, the affection held for friends and relatives. Finding someone on a census return tells me where they lived and how they worked. Their postcard takes me on a journey about train arrivals, the birth of a child, the frustrations of busy lives.

As well as learning about these new families, I've also become more connected with my own ancestry. The grocers, mill workers, miners, servicemen, quarrymen, beer-house keepers, are all part of my ancestry.

In today's world we share our news on social media. We upload our photos, make announcements, even end relationships. We send a text to let others know we're home, at work, waiting for a bus. Messages sent from a holiday arrive before the kettle at home boils. Writing and receiving a postcard was special – clicking 'send' will never allow future generations to save and treasure the words of their friends and family.

What's Next?

One of the chief complaints made by experienced genealogists who watch *Who Do You Think You Are?* is how easy the programme makes research appear. Certificates confirming the birth or marriage of an ancestor are miraculously presented to the impressed celebrity. Can it really be that easy? Yes and no.

Even once you have obtained the relevant index records to obtain a copy of a certificate it takes time to actually receive that magical piece of paper. Whoa! Index records? Have a look at Free BMD. It's a free to use website and it might help you locate the information needed to order your documents.

For my research I only obtained the death certificates of anyone who had died relatively young. When I presented my research for each postcard, finishing with the news that someone had died at a young age would leave both me and you questioning what had happened. Again, as with all this research, we are only presented with the facts – but a death certificate, in particular, does allow us further insight into a person's life and times – including the cause and place where the death occurred.

There are two options for the certificates: a copy sent out in the post or a PDF version sent out by email in about five days. For this research I went for the cheaper and often swifter version of a PDF.

I'm getting ahead of myself here. Let me take you through what was necessary to research a postcard – then you can see how you can apply that method to your own research.

Why not begin by writing down what you think you know. For example, as I've already mentioned, my father was always called John – by his parents, his friends and us, his family. You won't find him anywhere in the official system; no, his first name was registered as Arthur. So, with that knowledge, keep an open mind when you explore your own family – begin with what you think you know, then check it.

The majority of the postcards in this book were posted around 1911. Even so, it wasn't possible to trace some recipients and that's why genealogy is a love hate relationship.

Although I occasionally use the online site FindMyPast, all the trees I have created are within Ancestry's site. You will probably need to subscribe to a provider to access the records you need. At times you will see adverts for free access – perhaps for a weekend or to tie-in with a TV programme. Once you begin, they hope you complete enough during that free period to tempt you into paying a subscription.

So, let's go to my starting point: searching the 1911 census. This census was taken on the night of 2 and 3 April. It was completed by the head of the household and they listed everyone in the property that night.

Assuming there is a family, you will find the names of the parents, the length of time they have been married, and how many children the wife has had during that marriage – born, died, living. Then the other occupants will be listed. The occupations and place of birth are also recorded. You can see how useful this census is – matching the number of children to the mother's details is particularly important. However, you might recall more than one postcard story where I discovered that errors – deliberate or otherwise – were made.

Looking at what you already know about your own family, is it possible to find an ancestor in the 1911 census?

When I found the recipient of a postcard, I then worked back to 1901, 1891, etc. The dates of the census returns are:

6 June 1841
30 March 1851
7 April 1861
2 April 1871
3 April 1881
5 April 1891
31 March 1901
2 April 1911
19 June 1921 (not yet available)
29 September 1939 (register, not census)

Once I had completed that first branch I looked at the other records that were available: baptism, marriage, probate – they all add detail to the census returns. Remember, the censuses were only taken every 10 years and people move, marry and die beyond the confines of those anniversaries. Other records help fill in the gaps. It's worth remembering that someone can still evade our research – be born, live, marry and die, and still avoid being recorded in these online reports. Sometimes you will spot a sibling in a record – perhaps travelling, witness to a marriage, etc. – and that can help further your branches.

Because I was mainly interested in what had happened *before* the time of the postcards being sent, looking at the 1939 register usually came last. Many of the subjects of my research weren't alive in 1939 but I certainly found this document interesting. As well as listing people and their occupations, it also shows their date of birth – not their age at that time.

When you're viewing these records online it's too easy to accept what's before you. Don't just click away – you must verify what you find. For example, you may think a family member has an unusual name and would therefore be very easy to track. Wrong! Never assume you are following the correct person. See if you can confirm them with another detail. For instance, if you have them in 1901, living at an address, and they married fairly close to that year, look at their marriage details. Are they at the same address? Do the occupations of the couple and their fathers match with the details you have? Yes, people move. Yes, people change jobs. But are you making a person fit with what you want?

Once you begin creating your tree online, you will be provided with hints – suggestions about the person. Review them with caution. They may be based on existing trees that contain errors.

My advice moves through the process at a brisk pace because it can sometimes be a swift process. However, my research has centred on only two or three generations. Occasionally I went further, but not often. Going as far back as possible is, I suppose, the aim of most family historians. In my own case, in my maternal line, I have struggled. My great-grandmother was my great-grandfather's second wife. I've already explained about the error on the birth certificates – that the mother's maiden name is that of my great-great-grandmother who wasn't alive at the time. Once I discovered that error I was able to find out more but it's been a slow process. I can hear the registrar asking for the mother's maiden name, and my great-grandmother – especially with the first child – makes the mistake of providing her own mother's maiden name. I'm sure everyone who has researched their family has similar stories to share and scare you with!

Seeing the handwriting of your ancestors provides a wonderful connection and the same is true of actually seeing the original documents. To do that, you will need to visit the relevant archive. It's recommended by genealogists that you do not rely entirely on the information found online, and I would agree with that. Although it hasn't been necessary to do so for this book, I have visited several records offices for other projects. My first visit to the office in Taunton was a thrill – irrespective of the documents I looked at.

I recall a fellow family historian who was looking for a missing auntie. The lovely lady had lived next door to his family. Neither of his parents had a sibling and the man was baffled. With great sensitivity, the archivist explained to the man that, as there was no trace of her in his tree and no family member knew of this aunt, it might be that she was a neighbour, known to him as Auntie.

Joining a local family history society will open up your research methods and knowledge. They usually meet once a month and have guest speakers. The topics covered will include genealogy, of course, but they will also include a strong element of social history – adding details to your ancestors and their lives. Don't worry if you don't live in the area of your tree's research – I've never left a meeting feeling disappointed.

There are at least two magazines available that provide help and information about genealogy. *Who Do You Think You Are?* and *Family Tree* have slightly different content. *WDYTYA?* will include additional information to that which was included in an episode on TV. *Family Tree* tends to focus more on helping us solve our problems and develop our research skills. Both magazines regularly run offers whereby you can subscribe at a discounted rate. Facebook groups abound – offering tips, sharing news. Be careful which you join. They can become more of a distraction than a help! There's no reason why you can't go it alone – just be aware that help is available.

If you create a tree, do you want to share it with the world? Caution is needed here – not every member of your family will want their details added (although anyone alive is automatically set to 'private' in Ancestry's site). We all have a right to privacy and you may find you have cousins that are not so keen on their family's details being laid bare. It's for that reason I have not brought any trees in this book to their most recent generations. Also, they are set to private. They appear in searches in Ancestry, but cannot be accessed without my permission. I am happy to share that information – and have already done so – but only with family members.

You might discover distressing information and you must be sensitive to how others will react. A sibling of one my postcard subjects died, I thought, in an industrial accident. I decided to obtain his death certificate and found his cause of death was suicide – graphically described. That poor man died in the 1930s and had no children. His siblings had children and they may still be alive today – the next generation certainly could be. There's a difference between them researching their tree and discovering the details of their uncle's death in the privacy of their home, to reading about it in a book about

266

postcards.

I've already mentioned that new information is becoming available all the time – where you found nothing one month, a new search can provide you with a surprising link. That's certainly true with many of the stories I've included in this book. As I worked my way through the final version, ticking the names and dates back to the source documents, I found more information about Edith Pickford née Broughton's son, Norman Pickford (postcard 072099). I knew he had died during World War II, but this new information provided an image of his headstone and the details of how he and seven others had been killed. Research is never complete and I know there will always be new details to add to a tree – but I have to stop at some point, and that's with the publication of this book.

All of the cards have been added to a blog and you can view them – both sides – in colour. There are some stories for which I had several cards and have not included them all in this book; they are also on the blog. Please look at the relevant story and note the last three digits of its reference to find a particular card – or you can lose yourself for a few minutes and scroll through the complete collection. The link to the blog is in the About the Author section of this book on page 279.

Happy hunting!

Index of Names & Locations

A
Abbott, 260
Abenheim, 149
Acklington, 68
Aitken, 71
Alcombe, 113
Alfreton, 115
Allahabad, 128
Allen, 94, 169, 220
Almondbury, 66
Amman, 44
Andrews, 43
Armitage, 48
Armstrong, 68
Arscott, 82
Aspin, 75
Aspinall, 133
Astbury, 71
Aston, 35
Attleborough, 142
Aubert, 166
Australia, 17, 26, 128
Aveton Gifford, 103
B
Bacon, 43
Baden, 80
Baggley, 156
Baggott, 259
Baggs, 222
Bakewell, 71
Baldock, 253
Balham, 131, 230
Balkham, 226
Banks, 44
Bannockburn, 129
Barbados, 129
Bardle, 253
Barnes, 138
Barnes, Bowley, 57
Barnsley, 151
Barnstable, 228
Barrett, 236
Basham, 142
Basingstoke, 91, 250
Bath, 228, 256
Battersea, 22, 219
Batty, 148
Baxendale, 24
Baxter, 185
Bayley, 39
Bazeley, 28

Beacham, 107
Beaminster, 236
Beasant, 230
Bedford, 142
Bedfordshire, 86
Bees, 113
Beeston, 126, 174
Beford, 220
Belfast, 129
Belgium, 166, 259
Bell, 84
Benham, 28
Bennett, 140
Bennett, Wag, 234
Bennington, 231
Berkshire, 91
Bermondsey, 222
Berry, 166, 173
Berwick, 226
Betts, 220
Bideford, 228
Bilbao, 253
Billbrook, 113
Birchby, 226
Bird, 199
Birkenhead, 170
Birmingham, 259
Birsay, 253
Bisham, 91
Bishop, 146
Blackband, 51
Blackburn, 75
Blackheath, 124
Blackler, 103
Blackpool, 24, 196
Blake, 63
Blandford, 82
Blandford Forum, 82
Blundell, 166
Bockhampton, 209
Bodman, 9
Bolton, 122
Boon, 154
Bosley, 113
Bossington, 30
Botting, 158
Bournemouth, 12, 162, 250
Bourton-on-the-Hill, 120
Bowden, 214
Bowles, 209
Bradburn, 94
Bradford, 248

Brain, 131
Brampton, 68
Braunton, 56
Brentford, 148
Brett, 53
Brewer, 146, 216
Briad, 133
Briden, 228
Briggs, 151
Brighton, 198, 219,
Brighton and Hove, 219
Brimscombe West, 212
Brislington, 206
Bristol, 183, 206
Broadfoot, David, 261
Bromley, 180
Brook, 156
Brougham, 105
Broughton, 17, 188, 267
Broughton Gifford, 21
Brown, 170
Bruce, Robert the, 129
Brussels, 259
Buckinghamshire, 26, 99, 122, 142, 219, 224
Bude, 89
Budgen, 91
Burdge, 107
Burgess, 169
Burghclere, 59
Burkinshaw, 151
Burne-Jones, Sir Edward, 220
Burr, 236
Burrage, 136
Burton-on-Trent, 140
Burton-upon-Trent, 140
Bushill, 162
Bute, 192
Buttenshaw, 37
Button, 113
Byfleet, 91
Bywater, 173
C
Calladine, 26
Calstock, 103
Camberwell, 46
Cambridge, 220
Cambridgeshire, 84
Came, 89
Canada, 56, 77, 84, 154, 174, 204, 212, 214
Cannes, 194
Canterbury, 11
Carhampton, 113
Caribbean, 129

Carn Brea, 101
Carpenter, 180
Cartwright, 204
Caterham, 32
Cauvin, 253
Cerne Abbas, 209
Chaffey, 210
Chalford, 11
Chance, 219
Chandler, 86
Channel Islands, 133
Chapman, 230
Charles, 219
Chatteris, 84
Cheffey, 209
Chellington, 86
Chelmsford, 131
Chelsea, 9, 22, 146
Cheltenham, 244
Cherington, 198
Chesham, 219
Cheshire, 94, 120
Cheshurst, 228
Chesterton, 77
Chew Magna, 206
Chile, 53
China, 250
Chippenham, 64, 107
Chiseldon, 80
Chiswick, 133
Chown, 146
Christer, 239
Clapham Common, 21
Clapton Common, 180
Clarendon Park, 188
Clark, 49
Clarke, 43
Cleethorpes, 185
Clegg, 176
Cliff, Clarice, 260
Clifford, 80
Clinch, 194
Clissold, 11
Clitheroe, 75
Clough, 174
Clowne, 117
Coats, 82
Cobb, 201
Coke, 28
Collinge, 204
Cookham, 91
Cordukes, 128
Cornish, 97

Cornwall, 10, 63, 89, 103, 158
Countanch, 133
County Fermanagh, 188
County Kerry, 189
Coventry, 51, 162
Cowan, 84
Cox, 129, 136, 236
Cranborne, 146
Crapper, 151
Crapper, Thomas, 151
Creamer, 126
Crease, 256
Crewe, 120, 214
Crewkerne, 63
Crippen, Dr, 57
Crosby, 105
Crosland, 66
Cross, 56
Crouch, 124
Crystal Palace, 134
Cumberland, 68, 105
Cumloquoy, Jessie, 253
Cupit, 22
Curran, Dave, 219
Curtis, 84
Cushing, 17
Cyprus, 129
D
Dalkeith, 228
Danecroft, 28
Darlington, 94
Dartmouth, 133
Davidson, 256
Davy, 183
Dawkins, 26
Day, 21
Dean, 142
Denton, 140
Derby, 26, 43
Derbyshire, 115, 118, 166, 224
Deverell, 21
Devon, 22, 56, 103, 158, 209, 250
Dew, 24
Dewsbury, 154
Dickinson, 219
Dixon, 156, 226
Doncaster, 126
Dorchester, 56, 194, 209, 250
Dorking, 37
Dorset, 12, 18, 56, 82, 146, 162, 194, 209,
   236, 248, 250, 260
Douai, 72
Douglas, 68
Down, 103, 226

Dredge, 237
Drissell, 107
Drummond, Charles, 129
Dursley, 34
E
Ealing, 84
Eames, 30, 233
Earl, 68
Earnshaw, 176
East Ham, 233
East Orchard, 82
Eastbourne, 17, 158, 181, 222
Easterbrook, 97
Eaton, 113
Edinburgh, 61
Edmonds, 250
Edward VII, King, 51, 131
Egypt, 44
Ellard, 32
Elliott, 248
Elsworth, 156
Emerson, 109
Ephgrave, 140
Essex, 44, 109, 142, 233
Evans, 35
Exeter, 89,206
Exmoor, 30
Eyles, 86
F
Farrar, 248
Fawkes, Guy, 63
Fell, 185
Fergusson, 216
Fermanagh, County, 188
Fermor, 222
Field Dalling, 126
Finch, 146
Finchley, 28
Flux, 59
Ford, 28, 59, 158
Foreman, 144
Forest Gate, 233
Forster, 61, 154
Foster, 233
Fowkes, 115
Fox, 61
France, 11, 14, 72, 77, 129, 174, 246, 260
Freeman, 9, 63, 212, 216, 261
Freestone, 136
French, 89
Freshford, 9, 63
Friggens, 101
Frost, 128
Fugeman, 239

Fulham, 84
Fullard, 166
Fyson, 91
G
Gainsborough, 201
Gandell, 129
Gandy, 94
Gayler, 61
Gedling, 105
Geigermann, 149
Genze, 77
George V, King, 134
Germany, 77, 149, 239
Gibraltar, 244
Gifford, 21, 129
Gilbert, 80
Gilby, 198
Gill, 120, 138
Gladwin, Christine, 245
Glasgow, 174, 192
Gloucestershire, 9, 34, 120, 198, 212
Goodacre, 115
Goodship, 99
Goodwin, 122
Grainthorpe, 185
Grant, 131, 194
Grantham, 17
Grasmere, 94
Gravener, 209
Great Yarmouth, 53, 138
Green, 56
Greenfield, 158
Greenway, 122
Greenwich, 53
Grimsby, 109, 185, 230, 256
Grindleton, 75
Grindley, 68
Guernsey, 124
H
Haddy, 103
Hale, 109
Hall, 48, 117, 160
Halstead, 176
Hampshire, 17, 59, 84, 91, 216, 248, 250
Hampstead, 56, 61
Hampton, 214
Hancock, 34
Hansford, 236
Hanson, 75
Hardy, Thomas, 3, 209
Harlesden, 48
Harris, 261
Harrison, 124, 253
Harsant, 216
Hastings, 222

Hawley, 224
Hayward, 113
Haywards Heath, 169
Head, 68,128
Heaton, 248
Hellenburgh, 138
Heppenstall Crapper, 151
Herbert, 32
Hertfordshire, 111, 140, 198, 228, 253
Hett, 214
Highlands, The, 129
Hilton, 196
Hinchcliffe, 174
Hirschman, 149
Hobbs, 26
Hockney, 185
Hofsommer, 77
Holford, 61
Holme, 244
Holme Barnett, 244
Holt, 21, 176
Hooker, 162
Horn, 61
Horsfield, 173
Horsforth, 126
Horton, 39
Hoskins, 214
Hoskyns, Henry, 63
House, 209
Howard, 15
Hoy, 254
Hull, 156
Hullock, 105
Hume, 77
Hunt, 82
Hyde, 253
Hyde Park, 148
I
India, 124, 128, 140, 194
Inkberrow, 259
Invergowrie, 140
Inverness-shire, 128
Ipswich, 80
Ireland, 128
Irvinestown, 189
Isitt, 86
Isle of Wight, 26, 59, 146
Islington, 128
Iver, 122
J
Jackson, 75
Jagger, 204
James, 71, 101
Jane, 158
Jay, 136

Jefferies, 189
Jeffreys, 124
Jersey, 133
Jervis, 151
Johnson, 26, 115, 154
Johnstone, 224
Jones, 256
Jordan, 44
K
Kendall, Captain Henry, 57
Kenilworth, 72
Kennard, 236
Kensington, 128, 180, 198, 250
Kent, 21, 37, 124, 170, 180
Kerry, County, 189
Killamarsh, 117
King, 80, 148
Kingsbridge, 103
Kingston, 122
Kitchener, Lord, 253
Knight, 97
Knightsbridge, 128
Knowlwood, 176
L
Laird, John, 170
Laird, Macgregor, 170
Lamb, 53
Lambe, 84
Lancashire, 204
Langdon, 113
Langton Matravers, 250
Larne, 261
Lawrence, 32
Le Cronier, 133
Lea, 113
Leak, 173
Leary, 185
Leatherhead, 131
Leckhampton, 244
Leech, 204
Leeds, 173
Leesing, 201
Leicester, 188, 192
Leicestershire, 115
Leigh, 61
Leith, 54
Leonard, 260
Lewis, 212, 219
Lewisham, 124
Leyland, 196
Leyton, 198
Lilley, 144
Lincolnshire, 109, 185
Lindley, 66
Lingard, 259

Little Thurlow, 169
Liverpool, 26, 56, 120, 133, 169, 251, 256
Llandudno, 71, 120
Llanelli, 201
Lloyd, 72
London, 9, 21, 37, 46, 48, 51, 57, 77, 99, 128,
    131, 133, 142, 146, 148, 151, 162, 198, 222,
    230, 239, 250, 260
Londonderry, 99
Longdon, 198
Longstaff, 124
Lord, 176, 196
Lowestoft, 154
Luckraft, 103
Luscombe, 103
Luxemburg, 259
Lynch, 128
Lyness, 254
Lynmouth, 228
M
Madden, 43
Maidenhead, 120
Manchester, 17, 196
Marcus, 133
Market Rasen, 185
Marsh, 46, 236
Martin, 216
Massachusetts, 10, 53, 138, 192
Matthews, 236
Mayo, 219
McKee, 239
McLean, 128
Melbury Osmond, 194
Merthyr Tydfil, 120
Merton Park, 22
Middlesex, 61, 148
Millbrook, 59
Miller, 133
Milton, 113
Minehead, 30, 113, 228
Modbury, 103
Moffatt, 231
Monk, 261
Monmouthshire, 10
Montacute, 63
Moore, 66
Morden, 236
Morell, 30
Moreton-in-Marsh, 120
Mortimore, 89
Moseley, 117
Mounsey, 68
Mozambique, 46, 120
Mullins, 57
Muthill, 129

N
Nab Wood, 248
Nebraska, 237
Neilson, 192
Nettlecombe, 113
New South Wales, 128
New York, 10, 174
Newton, 94, 219
Noble, 207
Norfolk, 126, 136, 138, 142, 253
North Perrott, 63
Northampton, 32, 43
Northamptonshire, 30, 32, 44, 198, 224
Northcott, 103
Northwich, 94
Norton-sub-Hamdon, 224
Norwich, 136
Nottingham, 44
Nottinghamshire, 118, 174
O
Oakes, 66
Oare, 124
Oates, 250
Oban, 61
Old Basing, 91
Old Cleve, 113
Oldbury, 259
Oldham, 204
Ontario, 174
Openshaw, 196
Orde Ward, 17
Organford, 236
Orkney, 253
Ormskirk, 24
Osborne, 189, 260
Oundle, 198
Owen, 34
Oxford, 17, 91, 131
P
Paddington, 99
Page, 53
Pain, 142
Palestine, 44
Palmer, 198
Paris, 259
Park Corner, 91
Parker, 17, 154
Parsons, 236
Payne, 142
Peckham, 146
Pembridge, 14
Penarth, 224
Pennsylvania, 149
Penrith, 105
Perkins, 39, 224
Perthshire, 129

Peterborough, 144
Pettit, 24
Phelips, Sir Edward, 63
Phillips, 233
Pickford, 188, 267
Piddletrenthide, 236
Piggin, 136
Pirbright, 32
Platt, 129
Plymouth, 103, 230
Pogmoor, 152
Pogson, 66
Pointon, 126
Pollard, 209
Pook, 194
Poplar, 99
Port Said, 44, 250
Portesham, 236
Porthpean, 101
Portsmouth, 84, 217, 253
Powell, 24, 214
Preece, 120
Prince Town, 158
Princetown, 158
Prussia, 133, 149
Purnell, 21
Purves, 228
Pylle, 250
Pywell, 198
Q
Quayle, 176
Quebec, 57
Quinton, 14
R
Radcliff, 196
Radnor, 120
Ramsden, 66
Randall, 91
Reading, 44
Redland, 183
Redruth, 101
Reeve, 43, 180
Reffell, 39
Renouf, 133
Reynolds, 219
Rhodes, 214
Rhodes, Cecil, 246
Richards, 101
Richardson, 105
Riches, 122
Riggs, 209
Ripley, 43
Roadwater, 113
Roberts, 183
Rochester, 129
Rogers, 103

Rollings, 120
Roseblade, 71
Rottingdean, 220
Rouse, 138
Rudd, 117
Rugby, 43, 236
Russ, 63
Russell, 14
Russia, 133, 253
Rutherglen, 192
Rutter, 94
Rye, 17
S
Sahara, 244
Salisbury, 148
Salt, 49
Saltash, 10
Saltdean, 220
Sampson, Brook, 224
Samson, 216
San Francisco, 149
Sandown, 169
Saul, 245
Saxby, 59
Schwarzenegger, Arnold, 3, 234
Scotland, 51, 54, 129, 192, 228
Seaforth, 251
Sears, 162
Selworthy, 30
Seven Kings, 233
Seward, 99
Shaftesbury, 82
Shaldon, 89, 169
Shanklin, 26
Shapland, 224
Sharnbook, 86
Sharpley, 185
Shaw, 156, 192
Sheerness, 250
Sheffield, 117
Sherborne, 236
Sheringham, 126
Sherriff, 228
Shipbourne, 170
Shoreditch, 142
Shropshire, 120
Sinclair, 51
Skellington, 173
Slough, 39, 120
Silverdale, 77, 260
Silvester, 146
Simmond, 122
Smalley, 75
Smethwick, 260
Smith, 15, 21, 86, 122, 230
Snizort, 128

Somerset, 9, 30, 56, 63, 97, 107, 113, 206,
    224, 237, 244, 250, 256, 260
Somerville, 129
South Africa, 188, 245
Southampton, 59, 216
Southwark, 122
Spain, 245, 253
Speight, 173, 248
Speir, 129
Spiers, 71
Squance, 113
St Albans, 111, 162
St Columb Minor, 89
St Helier, 133
St Michaels, 256
Stafford, 46
Staffordshire, 10, 48, 51, 118, 140, 166, 189,
    198, 260,
Stainer, 56
Standrin, 111
Steers, 148
Stepney, 239
Stevenage, 228
Stevens, 194
Stilton, 99
Stinsford, 209
Stoat, 113
Stoke-on-Trent, 260
Stone, 51
Stonehouse, 9, 212
Stonygate, 188
Stranraer, 261
Stretton, 180
Stroud, 12
Stroudley, 72
Strutt, 128
Stuckly, 107
Summers, 206
Surrey, 37, 61, 63, 122, 194, 250
Sussex, 140, 169, 214, 236
Sutton Coldfield, 35
Swain, 10
Swanage, 162, 236, 250, 260
Swanston, 53
Swindon, 80, 160
Syrad, Kay, 181
T
Tatchell, 260
Taunton, 97, 113 266
Taylor, 151, 204, 220
Taylor, Elizabeth, 163
Teakle, 9
Teignmouth, 89
Thompson, 86, 136
Thomson, 51, 86
Thorn, 220

Thorseway, 185
Thurleigh, 86
Thursby, 201
Till, 115
Tims, 46
Tincleton, 209
Tintinhull, 63
Todmorden, 176
Tommins, 156
Tomson, 46
Tooting, 146
Torr, 166
Torquay, 250
Totton, 59
Toxteth, 120
Treliving, 230
Trenchard, 214
Triplow, 84
Trollope, Anthony, 194
Tucker, 63
Tunbridge Wells, 226
Tunnell, 163
Tupper, 124
Turner, 109
Turner, David, 202
Twyford, 28
U
Uckfield, 226
United States of America, 10, 138, 140, 149, 192,
    214, 219, 237
Utah, 154
Uxbridge, 122
V
Valters, 30
Vass, 111
Vernon, 51
Vessey, 198
Vignoles, 51
W
Wait, 59
Wakely, 236
Wales, 34, 99, 120, 128, 206, 212
Walker, 154,192
Walkeringham, 201
Wallington, 160
Walsall, 71
Wareham, 82 ,236 ,250
Warren, 136
Warrington, 94
Warth, 84
Warwickshire, 21, 236
Washington, DC, 140
Watchet, 113

Watford, 48
Watson, 142, 222
Wandsworth, 86, 131, 251
Webb, 28, 80
Well Bank, 109
Wells, 144, 188, 206
Welsh, 122, 204
Welwyn, 198, 246
Wenman, 233
West Indies, 129
West Riding, 126
Westbourne, 162, 248
Westminster, 128
Weston, 169
Whislay, 216
White, 21,162
White City, 131, 136
Whitley, 94
Whitstable, 21
Whittard, 34
Whitticks, 21
Whitwell, 166
Wickstead, 24
Widen, 30
Wilkinson, 120, 256
Williams, 30, 171
Willmott, 107
Willshaw, 259
Wilmot, Arthur, 170
Wilson, 131
Wiltshire, 21, 80, 148, 160, 250
Wimborne, 248
Windsor, 91
Wingate, 144
Winrow, 24
Winscombe, 244
Winslow, 26, 224
Wise, 26
Wood, 37
Wood Green, 77
Woodhead, 201
Woolverton, 10
Worksop, 166
Wormley, 111
Worth Matravers, 260
Wright, 80
Y
Yarmouth, 54
Yarpole, 120
Yatton, 107
Yeovil, 63, 97
Yorkshire, 28, 126, 151, 173
Young, 236

About the Author

Helen Baggott grew up in Swanage. Although she no longer lives in the seaside town, home is still in Dorset.

For as long as she can remember, she has always loved history and writing – one of her first pieces of non-fiction was a project about the Outer Hebrides island of St Kilda. Although she was only 12 years old, she dreamed that researching and writing would be a major part of her future life.

She has written for local magazines including *Dorset Life* and combines writing with her role as a freelance copy-editor.

Posted in the Past, says Helen, legitimises the hoarding of ephemera – 'just in case it will make a good story'.

As well as developing the next two books in the *Posted in the Past* series – *Second Delivery* and *Return to Sender* – Helen is editing her father's memoirs of his childhood in the Black Country.

Contact Helen by email: PostedInThePast@gmail.com
Facebook and Twitter: @PostedInThePast
View the postcards mentioned in this book in colour:
PostedInThePast.blogspot.com
For more information about talks and writing workshops:
www.stourcastle.co.uk

Made in the USA
Middletown, DE
01 June 2020